Hope

Tia DeNora

Hope

The Dream We Carry

palgrave
macmillan

Tia DeNora
University of Exeter
Exeter, UK

ISBN 978-3-030-69869-0   ISBN 978-3-030-69870-6   (eBook)
https://doi.org/10.1007/978-3-030-69870-6

Cover illustration: Arild Lillebø/Alamy Stock Photo

This Palgrave Macmillan imprint is published by the registered company Springer Nature Switzerland AG
The registered company address is: Gewerbestrasse 11, 6330 Cham, Switzerland

Det er den draumen me ber på
at noko vedunderleg skal skje,
at det må skje —
at tidi skal opna seg
at hjarta skal opna seg
at dører skal opna seg
at berget skal opna seg
at kjeldor skal springa —
at draumen skal opna seg,
at me ei morgonstund skal glida inn
på ein våg me ikkje har visst um.

It is the dream we carry
that something wonderful will happen
that it must happen —
that time will open up,
that the heart will open up,
that doors will open up,
that the mountain will open up,
that springs will burst —
that the dream will open up,
that one morning hour we will glide in
upon a bay we never knew was there.

—Olav H. Hauge

For the residents, care staff, family and friends at
Mountbatten Hospice, Isle of Wight, UK
and
Sunniva avdeling for lindrende behandling, Haraldsplass Diakonale
Sykehus AS, Norway

Preface

This book is for anyone who has ever hoped, who is hoping, who will hope. That probably includes anyone. My motivation to write about hope is connected to an on-going research project on musical and social care in late and end of life—the *Care for Music* project. My aim is to consider matters that might be relevant to carers, loved ones and others, such as (a focal point in our project) music therapists, who stand alongside and assist people approaching the end life. And, of course—though I hope I am not being presumptuous—I am also attempting to write something of relevance to people who are facing death (which, again, includes all of us down the line). And finally, because I think that talk about hope is and should be personal I will occasionally touch on some of the things I have hoped for myself.

But a book on hope, completed in November, 2020 (just after the 2020 US Election result), is, perhaps inevitably, prompted by large-scale events. Global issues—climate crisis, violence, hostility, pandemics, homelessness, displacement, racism and racial hostility, economic hardship, modern slavery, loneliness, anxiety, mental illness—all of these have intensified. This intensity underlines a global *need* for hope and a corresponding need to *confront* hope—what hope is and what can, and cannot, be achieved by hoping. This confrontation includes distinguishing hope from wishful thinking and simple optimism. For me, a sociologist with an interest in how things take shape in action, that project also includes understanding hope as a complex form of situated practice. Such understanding can, I think, develop our ability to conceptualise hope as a kind of activity while also shining some light on the question of how change happens. I am hoping that, if this book is able to contribute to the theory and discourses associated with hoping, it might also offer resources for people coping *in extremis*.

I am old enough to remember first-hand the civil rights activism of the 1960s in America, and the non-violent reformist vision of Martin Luther King Jr. I remember the riots of 1967 (I grew up near Newark, New Jersey). And I remember the 'Holy Week Riots' after King's assassination in April 1968. As I write this preface, all over the world people have been protesting against a long history of racial inequality and racial violence. And while I am no longer young (or even middle-aged), I hope I might remain 'young' enough to continue to hope for Doctor King's dream of non-violence, justice, cooperation, mutual aid, dialogue and, importantly for the argument of what follows, *creativity* (the importance of the dream). That 'dream', and the creative action it may inspire, is integral to any form of, in King's term, 'creative protest'. (King used the term, 'creative protest' to refer to the Greensboro students who took seats at the lunch counter in a Durham Woolworths.) Creativity is, I feel certain, a core requirement for effecting change, especially when that project is fraught with conflict and hardship.

Our current public health crisis serves as another case in point: we are still (in most parts of the world) in the midst of the 2020, Covid-19 virus pandemic. The pandemic has brought with it many challenges, and for some people and groups more so than others—'lockdown', sickness, fatalities, anxiety, poverty, hunger, enforced separation of loved ones (including the need to say final goodbyes to loved ones via video-link), isolation, disruption, 'fake news', rebellion, and supply shortages. But it has also revealed many human qualities and capacities—patience, cooperation, innovation, courage, and kindness. Within this situation, and in particular in the 'post-apocalyptic' discussions of what will happen 'after

C-19 (comparisons being made to 9/11, to the Lisbon Earthquake, to the plague), conversations are taking shape around what a potential 'new normal' could, or should, include, in relation to the environment, alternative economies, consumerism, global health, all of which are framed as hopes.

Shortly after the start of the C-19 pandemic and the lockdowns in most European countries, on March 23, 2020, the Swiss alpine town of Zermatt began to display work by light artist Gerry Hofstetter. Postings of these images have since circulated widely in the media. Some of the images contain public service messages (for example, 'stay home'), others national flags from across the world. But in one of them, the Matterhorn's peak is bathed in red, the message in bold white letters spelling only one word—*hope*. In relation to the cultural imagery of hope (discussed in Chapter 1) and Goethe's meteorology as discussed in Chapter 5 ('Moving Mountains') I believe the image is apt. As Goethe observes, the mountains are by no means 'dead' (unmoving, unmovable). On the contrary, they respond to the environment and undergo metamorphosis. As I will describe, hope is part of the methodology for changing the social landscape. For this reason, hope is, in the words of Norway's most famous poem, 'the dream we carry'.

Exeter, UK   Tia DeNora

Acknowledgments

My first thanks is to my long-term research collaborator, Professor Gary Ansdell. It was Gary's writings on hope in *How Music Helps* (2014—discussed in Chapter 4) and conversations around that work that kindled the thoughts developed here. At one stage, Gary and I discussed writing this book together and many of the ideas here have come out of conversations about music and time (and I thank him also for permission to quote from his reflections linked to our current joint research). It was also Gary (and the late Mercédès Pavlicevic) who introduced me to Goethe and his 'gentle methods' which feature largely in the final chapter here. Our shared interest in the poetics of knowledge and Goethe's 'gentle empiricism' is continued in our collaborative writing and forthcoming work, and in our memories of Mercédès.

I also owe thanks to three project teams. First, to the AHRC Care for Music project team which, in addition to Gary Ansdell, includes (in the UK) Heather Edwards and Fraser Simpson and (in Norway at the University of Bergen) Randi Rolvsjord and Wolfgang Schmid. Within the Care for Music, project we have worked alongside people who, despite living with serious illness or living without, so-called, 'mental capacity', nonetheless have found ways of being that contain meaning, pleasure, and joy, if not always hope. We have been exploring how engagement with music features in that process, and in ways that reverse the usual 'music for care' problematic. Thanks to the Arts and Humanities Research Council of the United Kingdom for funding for this work (Grant Ref: AH/S003592/1). Thanks also to the interdisciplinary team of the MARCH Network, led by PI Daisy Fancourt—Helen Chaterjee, Kamaldeep Bhui, Paul Crawford, Geoffrey Crossick and Jane South. The MARCH project promotes research on community engagement, social assets and mental health and thus speaks directly to hope and its production in social contexts. During the Covid-19 pandemic, that project adapted to turn its attention to digital resources for being together and being creative, and the interrelationship between participation in creative activity and mental health during difficult times. Thanks also to the ARC Discovery Project on Social cohesion and resilience through intercultural music engagement, PI Jane Davidson and Mariko Hara, research assistant in Norway.

Thank you to Sharla Plant and Liam Inscoe-Jones, Preetha Kuttiappan at Palgrave Macmillan, and Poppy Hull, formerly at Palgrave Macmillan. Thanks to five anonymous reviewers for their very constructive criticism, suggestions and support. Through them I have learned new literatures; their scholarly generosity has considerably enriched this book. Thanks also to students and colleagues within SocArts at Exeter, and to my husband Douglas S. Tudhope not only for his intellectual support but, in the case of this book, for a lot of cooking and bringing meals upstairs when an injured knee meant I was involuntarily barred from kitchen duty. I am indebted to the lively Ph.D. research seminar at Nordoff Robbins London, the 'Alliance' Symposium in Gentle Methods (Jo Parsons organiser), the Glasgow Improvisers Orchestra and the research project team around that group led by Raymond MacDonald (Robert Burke, Ross Birrell, Maria Sappho Donohue). Special thanks also to Raymond MacDonald for technical advice on circular breathing as discussed in Chapter 5. Thanks to Stiftinga Det Norske Samlaget for permission to quote in full what is often described as Norway's most famous poem, Olav H. Hauge's beautiful, '"Det er den draumen"/It is the dream'. Thanks, also, to students and colleagues at the Grieg Academy,

University of Bergen—*sakte, sakte, kanskje en dag, jeg håper å glida inn på et språk me ikkje har visst um.* And finally, thank you to the two hospices who are the dedicatees of this book. Their work is vitally important for people who are confronting the end of life or loss of loved ones. It is a privilege to learn from you about what it can mean to have and practice careful hope.

Contents

1

Hope: A Critical Introduction

In the face of hardship people *hope*—for better times and for signs that suggest that hope is justified. As the opposite of despair, hopefulness is also the bedrock of creative and non-violent change. While hope involves an emotional stance or style (emotion being understood as affective orientation and readiness to act), it is also different from other emotions and affective stances in important ways. Unlike, for example, joy or sorrow, where an actual object—a person, an event, a perception or thought—gives rise to emotion, hope is an emotional orientation to something that is desired but that has not (yet) happened. Indeed, we may hope for things that may never happen. In this sense hope and longing are often intertwined.

Thus, hope is future-oriented, although in a unique way. There are other emotion-laden orientations that take shape in relation to desired future events—anticipation and expectancy, for example. Anticipating or expecting something 'good' is a 'happy' orientation. I can take pleasure in, and enjoy, for example, looking forward to being reunited with a loved one after a lengthy journey. I can enjoy looking forward to attending a long-awaited event—a live concert after a long period during which concert attendance was impossible (as it is now during Covid-19

T. DeNora, *Hope*,
https://doi.org/10.1007/978-3-030-69870-6_1

pandemic of 2020). In both of these cases, my anticipation is tinged with hope—I hope that nothing goes awry with my travel plans; I hope that concerts will return. So too, I may expect that, later today the rain will stop, that I will go for a walk, that you or someone else might suggest walking with me. Again, I might say, 'I hope to get out for a walk later on'. But in these cases, my hopes are supported with more than a little expectation, just as I might say, 'I hope to cook something nice for lunch today'. The difference, then, between anticipation and expectation on the one hand, and hope on the other hand, is that the former take shape with a degree of certainty—I am looking forward to things that have a *likelihood* of happening. There is little anxiety about whether these things will occur. By contrast, with hope, there is often a great deal of anxiety, indeed often anguish, about whether what one hopes for will ever actually transpire.

To take a relatively trivial, but personal, example (and one that did not seem trivial to me at the time): I have just spoken that I might 'expect' to take a walk later today. Some months ago, I injured a knee and for more than four weeks, when the pain was fairly intense, I was unable to walk and could not leave the upstairs level of our two-story house. During that time, which coincided with the period of the Covid-19 lockdown (which was in some ways fortuitous, since I could not actually go anywhere anyway) I sat up, mostly in bed with the laptop, worked, and hoped—fervently hoped—that I would eventually get back outdoors for a walk. I confess that hope was sometimes tinged with more than a little self-pity, and sometimes with a mild dose of despair as I thought about how I am no longer a young person and how joints in the 'over-sixties' (sic) do not always properly heal.

I was fortunate—the knee healed, just as all the diagnostic sites on the web (that I, somewhat obsessively, consulted) said it would. (There was no possibility of visiting a doctor or physical therapist at that stage of the lockdown.) I am mobile again (Nordic walking poles helped a lot) and in retrospect I can see how hoping helped me cope with this, relatively minor, setback. But not everyone is as lucky, in terms of being mobile— or otherwise. I thought it was ironic, but also a resource, that, at that time I was beginning to write a book about hope I gained additional first-hand experience of what it feels like to hope while in pain. That experience offered an object lesson in what it might mean to speak of hope arising in the face of difficulty, constraint, or pain. I hoped for my knee while, at the same time, and just like everyone else, I also hoped for an end to the pandemic and that the virus would not affect too many people unduly.

This simple example (yet further simplified for this telling) show-cases some of the defining features of what hope is, and is not. While hope involves a kind of anticipatory consciousness, it is something more complicated than anticipation or expectancy per se, and there is a rich philosophical tradition that distinguishes hope from expectation (Bloeser and Stahl 2017). The latter is characterized by, as Alan Petersen describes (2015: 12), a predictive feature; we come to 'expect' things we think are supported by past experience, things that will 'probably' happen, and that we expect because, empirically speaking, they are likely. I might speak casually about what I 'hope' to cook, but past experience, coupled by what is in the refrigerator or the garden, might mean that what I really mean is that I am expecting to cook that specific thing, or something like it, later.

In the discussions that follow, I am mostly not going to be writing about these 'pleasant' forms of hoping and the (pleasant) hopes that conjoin hope, anticipation, and expectation. I will, however, consider the matter of hope's social distribution—who can and cannot entertain pleasant forms of hope and the inequalities associated with who may hope for what—and the question of who has food in the refrigerator and can think about what to cook for dinner is an urgent example of this matter. I am also not, for the most part, considering more 'ordi-nary' hoping, as richly attended to by Julie Brownlie (2014). Brownlie describes what we might think of as bourgeois mundane hopes, for example how as part of our 'being there' in daily life, we may 'hope', when checking into a hotel, to get a room with a view. (Brownlie considers the hilarious consequences of an unrealistic, and rather petty, hope for a room with a view, as presented in one episode of the comedy series, *Faulty Towers* [2014: 53].)

That is mostly not what this book is about. Occasionally, I will examine hoping in 'nice' circumstances, but I am mostly concerned with the kind of hope that is invoked in response to dire and troubled times.

The hopefulness and forms of hoping examined in what follows are imbued with uncertainty; the 'better' futures to which they orient may be impossible to gauge. In this sense hope differs from faith; the latter involves a kind of certainty, and sometimes an expectant certainty even in the absence of empirical indicators: I may have faith in, for example, the idea of life after death, salvation, hell, purgatory, and so on. Whereas, if I am 'terminally ill', I may nonetheless, as described by the death and dying scholar, Elisabeth Kübler Ross, hope that I might, 'wake up one morning to be told that the doctors are ready to try out a new drug' (2009: 113). As Kübler Ross puts it, this kind of hope both acknowledges the reality of what is probably going to happen (there is no faith that one will be 'cured') while remaining open to the possibility that something wonderful will happen. This openness, Kübler Ross suggests, keeps spirits buoyant, helps people to endure what must be endured and—importantly as I will explore momentarily when I consider the role of dreaming and fantasy in relation to hope—provides, 'a form of temporarily needed denial' (Kübler Ross 2009: 113) that in turn may help to keep us on the lookout for possibilities and resources that can lead to change. Hope is, in other words, more empirically alert than is faith.

Thus, hope is a vigilant emotional orientation and as such, I shall suggest that hope is integral to what Gene Sharp calls the, 'methods' of non-violent action (of which Sharp lists 108 [Sharp 1973]). Hope recognises that what is hoped for may not happen, yet it pursues signs of the possible alleviation or transcendence of present (difficult) circumstances. As I will describe later, hope fuels the pursuit of what some might call, 'wiggle room'—space for possibility. This focus on, and longing for, change, and change in the earthly world, is what keeps hope in the forefront of philosophies and interdisciplinary studies of trauma, health and illness, resistance, dissidence, protest and dissent.

Not knowing what will happen down the line while imagining what might be possible and being on the lookout for how to effect those possibilities, hopefulness—being hopeful—is a highly creative way of being, a central point to all that follows in this book. To hope, whether privately or collectively, is to possess a utopian vision, an imagined vision (or 'dream') of a place, time or state in which things are, if not perfect, then certainly better. Hope is 'creative' then because it entails much more than a an emotion or 'readiness for action'. By contrast, hope *is* action: to hope is to act and hope as action produces a content-rich, practical orientation to the future. This is to say that a hopeful person is someone who is acting and orienting in relation to specific things— she or he has an object or a vision of what the future can, could, might, should, and possibly, will entail. Hope, then, involves practical action. It involves imagining and longing for a hypothetical, *better* reality and actively pursuing that reality. It is in this sense that hope is utopian. In the next chapter I will develop what I see as hope's crucial relationship to dreaming (understood as envisioning a better reality), a relationship articulated in detail by the most significant theorist of hope in the twentieth century, philosopher Ernst Bloch.

1.1   Ernst Bloch and Hope as Dreaming

Bloch devoted three volumes to the topic of hope and another volume to utopian thought. His work continues to serve as the touchstone for hope studies and it has been inspirational to critical theorists. While my discussion in these chapters will not be overtly philosophical (I am trained as a sociologist and a music sociologist but not as a philosopher), no book on hope can ignore Bloch's perspective.

Bloch is concerned with, 'thinking beyond the present' and— supremely—upon imagination and dreaming. Bloch contrasts hoping to a more passive orientation to the world as it is, as if things—conditions, circumstances, situations—simply 'are'. This passive approach is seen as leading in turn to a form of reification, a failure to recognize reality as an historical production, made in and through concerted social activity. In other words, Bloch's conception of hope is one that emphasizes hope as an activity, or as involving active perception. This vision of hope has, in different ways, been articulated across the social sciences and humanities (for example, see Morgan 2016 on this seam in philosophy and sociology).

Bloch addresses these matters at some length in volume one of his treatise on hope. There, he describes how creative dreaming, specifically daydreaming, is integral to hope, hoping understood as an orientation to the 'not yet conscious' (Bloch, vol. 1: 11). This dreaming is what makes hope 'creative' and also potentially able to transcend present realities, and present troubles; it involves the production of an imagined 'otherness'. Hope is thus an orientation to things (often unclear, not articulated) that stand outside of ongoing conditions; it entails a pre-conscious, 'venturing beyond'. As former President Barack Obama put it, hope is characterized by an audacity, a tenacity and commitment to a dream in the face of all or any evidence to the contrary.

Hope's mixture of dreaming, longing, waiting and watching mean that it is often depicted as vulnerable, fragile, enduring. These qualities are captured by hope's metaphors, which have systematically been considered by psychologists, including in cross-cultural context (Averill et al. 1990). The predominant imagery is drawn from nature. It includes glimmers of light (e.g., 'at the end of the tunnel', or 'darkest before dawn'), tender green shoots, and, perhaps most famously, birds, as in Emily Dickinson's hope as, 'the thing with feathers'. But if hope is depicted as fragile it is also understood as something durable, for example, through the metaphor of mountains (Martin Luther King's 1964 Nobel Peace Prize Lecture, for example, spoke of how our, 'valley of despair' could be transformed into 'new peaks of hope'). Thus, hope's metaphors underline its particular and paradoxical feature—simultaneously fragile *and* resilient, miniscule *and* vast. This paradox is, I will suggest, part of hope's power and its understanding from within as a fifth metaphor—an anchor in turbulent times.

1.2   Hope in Culture

In most of the world's religions, hope is understood as a means of spiritual fortification. In the Qur'ān, believers are exhorted to follow Jacob's example and '*never give up hope of raḥma [the mercy] of Allah. Certainly no one despairs of Allah's raḥma, except the people who disbelieve*' (12:87). Similarly, in the Christian tradition, hope is viewed as a source of psychological and spiritual security and for this reason it is associated with the symbol of an anchor. Hope *stabilises*—a ship, people, the church, faith—so that these things are not swept away in the face of turbulence:

> hope we have as an anchor of the soul, both sure and steadfast, and which entereth into that within the veil [i.e., hope allows us to remain secure and enter into God's presence]. (Hebrews 6:19, King James Version)

Similarly, hope is linked, within Judiasm, to holding people fast, whether in the face of a certainty that a better future will arrive (messianic hope), or yearning (*tocheles*), or even hope despite the certainty that things may never improve (*tikvah*).

That said, some religious traditions reject this understanding and role of hope. In some accounts of the Buddhist tradition importance is placed by contrast on the need to renounce hope (to become totally 'tired out' and to cast away yearning). The suggestion here is that only then can we be strong:

> [w]ithout giving up hope – that there's somewhere better to be, that there's someone better to be – we will never relax with where we are or who we are. (Chödrön: 38)

Despite these differences, religious traditions seem to share the assumption that hope is nobler and more complicated than simple optimism. Simple optimism, understood as the casual assumption that, 'something will turn up' (which is sometimes termed the Micawber principle after the character in Charles Dicken's novel, *David Copperfield*), is related to 'Pollyannaism' (looking for the good in any situation no matter how dire).

In addition, depending upon its format, simple (uncritical) optimism can be destructive. As Lauren Berlant (2011) has suggested, we may become strongly attached to unrealistic visions of 'the good life' and in ways that can be detrimental to flourishing. For example, we may genuinely believe in the prospect of upward mobility, meritocracy, the 'American dream' or, perhaps, the idea that a particular political figure might, 'make America great again'. According to Berlant, attachments such as these, just as attachments to excessive quantities of fat and sugar, alcohol cigarettes (or, one might add, the opposite—obsessive concern with diet and cleanly eating in pursuit of 'health' or 'beauty'), are part of the 'slow death' arising from a discriminatory and exploitive American economic environment in which people enter upon the vicious cycle of 'self-medication', unhealthy consumption, and fantasy-attachments so as to get through the day, the week, the month (2011: 116). This need to 'get through' must not however be dismissed but rather studied empathetically and sociologically. As Berlant puts it:

> How do we think about labor and consumer-related subjectivities in the same moment, since, in my view, one cannot talk about scandals of the appetite - along with food, there's sex, smoking, shopping, and drinking as sites of moral disapprobation, social policy, and self-medication - without talking about the temporality of the workday, the debt cycle, and consumer practice and fantasy? (2011: 105)

These forms of optimism are linked to what journalist Roz Coward (1985) memorably described as constituting a cycle of desire/dissatisfaction. Optimistically, we locate desired objects, form attachments—to a new lipstick, flavor of ice cream, diet, or, indeed, person—in the hope that things will improve (desire)/and we are once again disappointed when they do not (dissatisfaction) and so/we form a new attachment (desire)—and the cycle continues.

As forms of wishful thinking these things pass as 'self-care' or 'self-medication', distraction, and deception; they are antithetical to what Timo Jütten, presenting the work of Jonathan Lear, speaks of as 'radical hope' (2006). Jütten outlines how this more radical form of hope is akin to Theodor Adorno's understanding of, as he saw it, human beings' 'metaphysical need' for hope and Adorno's understanding of the dangers of misplaced, or blind, optimism (Jütten 2019). Adorno, Jütten argues, considered that 'radical hope' was only possible when we are willing to confront the very worst possible scenarios and conditions. As Jütten puts it, this means that hope, 'comes after despair has been worked through' (Jütten 2019: 295). Indeed, Adorno's focus on the culture industry can be understood precisely as a critique of its distraction from confronting the worst squarely and therefore diagnostically in terms of a serious desire for a better world:

> Any attempt to give people hope that avoids squaring up to our predicament manipulates them: 'They are treated by metaphysics in fundamentally the same way as by the culture industry'. (Jütten 2019: 295)

In short, simple or uncritical optimism can be 'cruel' and it can involve self-deception (so-called 'blind optimism' and 'wishful thinking'). And while hope does involve a kind of optimism, it is not optimism per se. Radical, or true, hope, in both Lear's and Adorno's sense, is more honest; more critical; it is informed, seeks to come to terms with, the worst possible, and yet maintains a longing for a better world or situation. In this sense, hope is often understood to be 'tragic' (Eagleton 2015). Hope is 'tragic' because it refuses to relinquish a dream, even when it may seem clear that the chances of realizing a dream may be very low (Ehrenreich 2009: 4).

1.3   Assessing Hope

Hope is therefore a restless, stubborn thing and for these reasons the philosopher Nietzsche, considering the Pandora myth, viewed hope as the worst of all evils:

> that jar which Pandora brought was the jar of evils, and he [humankind] takes the remaining evil for the greatest worldly good—it is hope, for Zeus did not want man to throw his life away, no matter how much the other evils might torment him, but rather to go on letting himself be tormented anew. To that end, he gives man hope. In truth, it is the most evil of evils because it prolongs man's torment. (Nietzsche 1984: 58)

For Nietzsche, hope was cruel, in a way that resonates with Berlant's (2011) perspective on optimism that I have just considered. To hope, in Nietzsche, is to remain trapped in a cycle of hope/endurance/torment/hope, in other words, a state of nervous tension and anxiety, forever awaiting what might never occur. Hope is here understood as a vigilant, if futile, form of attention.

If hope has been understood as a torment, it has also been understood, within the social history of religion, as a strategy of power, and a way to encourage behavioral quiescence. At different times, in different religions, hope, or rather, arguably, the wrong kind of hope, has been encouraged deliberately to counter the idea that taking worldly action is worthwhile or effective. '[God] does not adopt all promiscuously to the hope of salvation', Jean Calvin wrote, 'but gives to some what he denies to others', in Calvin's words (2008: 607). Here, hope, that one is part of the elect and will therefore achieve salvation in the afterlife is, however fervent, not dissimilar to trust in the will of another (the deity), perhaps encouraged by earthly signs of predetermination such as prosperity (Weber 2011).

Along similar lines, in seventeenth century Salem (Massachusetts), in the face of the belief in an all-powerful deity, attempting to take worldly or material action was viewed a form of devilry (at the heart of the Salem witch trials was a kind of movement against women's folk-medical nous, for example the brewing of herbal tisanes to cure a pox or fever, which was seen as a kind of meddling against the will of god [Reed 2007]). Within this purview hope is antithetical to, disconnected from action. One can, 'only hope' that it shall be god's will that a fever abates, or that a virus is not fatal. The possibility of action is curtailed.

Linked to these critiques, hope is often rejected within programs of protest and civil disobedience because it is seen to be numbing and productive of passivity (Terpe 2014). As climate-activist Greta Thunberg famously put it, 'I don't want you to be hopeful. I want you to panic' (Foer 2019). Seen through this lens, hope is a distraction from more practical and activist pursuits. Within this purview, it is only when hope dies, when it is replaced with hope's opposite, despair, and when despair is in turn replaced with anger, that action—activism—properly can begin.

For these reasons, thinkers of many varieties have held mixed views on hope. In particular, hope's link to dreaming is often regarded as unstable and dangerous. As Susan Buck-Morss (2002) puts it in her study, *Dreamworlds*, in relation to critical theory and in particular Bloch and Adorno, dreaming is at once central to the 're-enchantment' of the world, in the sense that it quickens the imagination and serves as a precursor to critical engagement, *and* it is dangerous. Dreaming is dangerous because it can be manipulated, its energy harnessed in ways that produce negative and/or detrimental desires associated with domination or exploitation (Buck-Morss 2002: xi). In Bloch's words, 'images can be held down and misused' (ibid.: 14) and in ways that lead to failed and misplaced utopian visions and failed utopias is a regular theme in studies of health technologies (Petersen 2015) and social reform. (For explication and a genealogy of the utopia concept see Levitas 2010 [1990]. For a history of utopia see Claeys 2020.)

There is a strong scholarly tradition devoted to the history of 'failed' utopias, intentional communities, and dystopias (Claeys 2017). That history considers failed prophesy (Jenkins 2013; Festinger 2009), communal ideals that fail when put into practice. The question of how these 'failures' are identified, by and for whom, is of vital importance (did the Obama presidential election offer utopian promise? Has the Trump regime consolidated the failure of that utopia or has it sought to pursue a different—and, as many suggest—'bad' form of utopian vision, a dystopia?).

Throughout history and today, there are, what we might term, negative hopes, instances and eras where, for example, individuals and groups have formed attachments to authoritarian politicians to whom they impute messianic forms of identity. As we shall see presently, hope has for this reason and others, inspired a raft of criticism and has been cast in opposition to wellbeing and to activism. It is vital therefore to examine critically hope's cultural resources and to consider the question of where hopes imaginary, its dreams and visions come from, and how they take shape. It is equally vital to examine how hopes may be captured by powerful interests. The cultural structures and political-economic relations of hoping is a topic both for research and public awareness.

For example, as I will describe in more detail in Chapter 3 (and in dialogue with Kübler Ross [2009] on hope in terminal illness), in relation to 'miracle' cures and technologically-articulated hope, hope cannot be considered independent of political economic systems where hope may be aligned with power and an often-rich array of profit motives.

There are also equally critical issues associated with the ethics of hoping and what is hoped for. One may hope for things that others might abhor—things that are discriminatory or that involve domination. One may hope for vengeance, revenge, annihilation, the misfortune of one's 'enemies'. Moreover, forms of hoping, and things hoped for, may be more or less accessible to different groups and individuals and hope—its basis, the feeling that it is 'worth' hoping and investing the energy into hoping—may be distributed along lines that divide people into racial, ethnic, gendered, ageist, dis/abled, look-ist (and many other) categories, though the discriminatory patterns of hope and hope's objects is or can be subject to change—in relation to direct action and to circumstance. For example, even as recently as twenty years ago, it might well seem 'not worth' investing hopeful energy in the idea of running for President of the United States if one were African American or a woman (or indeed, a white male real estate mogul with no prior experience of governance).

But critical assessments of hope, such as these, while important to bear in mind, are also too general. They are not clarified with reference to particular realms, dreams, and contexts of hoping. For example, climate activists suggest that in relation to climate change, there is much that can be done—there are opportunities for action now (even if just what should be done is contentious). It might, therefore, seem perfectly reasonable to suggest that action, rather than hope and longing, are to be desired in the realm of climate change. In the same way, if I break a bone, I will probably want medical attention rather than simply hope that the bone will heal.

However, there are other realms, and other times, where it may be, or seem to be, nothing that can be done. The reasons why nothing can be done will vary. They may be connected to forceful restraint, lack of means, concern for the knock-on effects of what realising one's hopes might entail, or—and this will be crucial to the argument that follows—insufficient imagination, individual or collective. At these times, and in these kinds of circumstances, arguably, hope, because it involves a close attention to the present and a search for signs and opportunities, can play a vital role and I explore this point in Chapter 2, and Chapter 5 where I will suggest that this form of attention is connected to hope's strong creative capacity and thus hope's method and technique. So, the varying assessments of hope—a torment, a sedative, a palliative remedy, or an important activity for change—need to be considered in relation to the varying contexts within which hoping, *as an activity*, takes place, and in relation to what is hoped for and how hope is critiqued.

Those contexts and the social relations of hoping found within them are in turn linked to other critical considerations of hope and hoping, overtly sociological and linked to wider contexts such as the institutional and economic arrangements under which hope occurs. These critiques revolve around how hope has been exploited as an instrument of power and, as Foucault (1991) initially called it, 'governmentality'. The term 'govern'-'mentality' means precisely what that compound spells out—a way of governing or managing people's outlooks—their mentalities (which include emotions and impulses) through the circulation of patterned ways of thinking and speaking, images and forms of 'expert advice'. As Novas (2006), Rose (2007) and Rose and Novas (2005) have described, hope can be easily absorbed into biopolitics; it needs to be considered in terms of its role within political economies (Novas 2006; Good et al. 1990). For example, patient groups may be captivated by and encouraged to voice hopes for advanced technological and medical solutions to pathologies which are linked to biomedical and biomedical-commercial interests. Hope can, in other words, be managed, and as such hope is part of what is described as the sociology of expectation (Novas 2006: 291) what, according to our horizons of experience and the ways they take shape and can be shaped by external conditions, we come to hope for and how we identify the objects of our hopefulness. There are, in short, 'regimes of hope' (Moreira and Palladino 2005) within which discourses of hope are harnessed to imaginaries of 'miracle' cures, wonder drugs and/or compliance with mainstream procedures that may be unrealistic or inappropriate for some forms of illness and some people and yet serve the interests of specialist sectors (corporate or entrepreneurial). The social, political and economic relations of hoping must be examined carefully, in other words, if hope is not to become part of what Barbara Ehrenreich once termed the, 'cult of positivity' (Ehrenreich 2009) and the turn away from realism.

1.4   Specifying Hope

How we assess hope *depends*—on the realm in which hope takes shape, on the person, on social circumstances, on wider contexts and conditions, on resources and, as we shall explore later, on specifically what is hoped for, and on the politics of how that object is articulated. It is here where the 'what' of what is hoped for becomes an important object of small-p politics, and therefore critical inquiry.

In real life and, importantly, in real time, hope and hoping are complicated—in terms of how they are experienced and in terms of their effects. Hope may deflect attention, it may be unrealistic (though who defines this is important). Hope may blind us to grim realities, it may take us away from action—and yet nonetheless, in particular situations or at particular times, hope may be of utmost importance. In all of these cases, though, hope must also be located in context of all the other ways of being and feeling that it is possible to experience at any given time; hope and despair, for example, may be experienced simultaneously, alternating, in split-second flashes and clouding action with ambivalence and mixed motivation.

Finally, perhaps it is more interesting, and more useful, to situate hope not simply as an emotional *predisposition* to act but *as* activity involving specific people in time and place and oriented to a wide, and possibly fluctuating, range of objects, things to be hoped for, and circumstances affecting the present and future. Considering hope's situations opens up hope to empirical investigation and in ways that privilege the meanings and values of those who do the hoping.

Many questions can then be posed and throughout this book I add what I consider to be questions for further research. For example, what are we doing when we hope? What does that process involve in space and over the long and short durée? What kinds of things become hope's objects, which is to ask, where do the dreams of hope originate, what do people hope for and how do hope's objects sit in relation to social relations, culture, and practical circumstances? How do people hope, which people, when, and where and when do people not hope, about what, when, where, why and with what resources? If we consider hope as *hoping*, and in ways that are grounded in actual situations, scenes, and circumstances, and if we consider hope in relation to actual people, perhaps we can begin to elucidate what hope actually does—its actual place within our lives and in relation to specific features of our lives. And perhaps we can also explore where hope comes from, when and how it is generated, its history of production and deployment of resources from scene to scene across a moment, a life, an era, a social group.

To these ends, in this book I ask how and under what circumstances do situations of hoping and/or despair assume specific forms, involve particular practices, and how do these forms and practices affect possibilities, and opportunities for, experience? Perhaps most intriguingly, I will also seek to address the question of how, if at all, hoping is linked to actual change (tiny perhaps invisible changes and larger, more dramatic changes), when, where, what kind, and for whom. What, in other words, can hope achieve? Pursuing these questions, I suggest, refreshes the topic of hope, and refreshes hope as an important human activity. How, then, to develop an empirically oriented, situated understanding of hoping as a form of activity?

References

Averill, J., Caitlin, G., & Chon, K. K. (1990). *The Rules of Hope*. New York: Springer Verlag.

Berlant, L. (2011). *Cruel Optimism*. Durham, NC: Duke University Press.

Bloeser, C., & Stahl, T. (2017). Hope. In E. N. Zalta (Ed.), *The Stanford Encyclopedia of Philosophy* (Spring 2017 ed.). Retrieved on June 20, 2020 from https://plato.stanford.edu/archives/spr2017/entries/hope/.

Brownlie, J. (2014). *Ordinary Relationships: A Sociological Study of Emotions, Reflexivity and Culture*. Basingstoke: Palgrave MacMillan.

Buck-Morss, S. (2002). *Dreamworld and Catastrophe: The Passing of Mass Utopia in East and West*. Cambridge, MA: MIT.

Calvin, J. (2008). *Institutes of the Christian Religion* (H. Beveredge, Trans.). Peabody, MA: Hendrickson's Publishers.

Claeys, G. (2017). *Dysutopia: A Natural History*. Oxford: Oxford University Press.

Claeys, G. (2020). *Utopia: The History of an Idea*. London: Thames and Hudson.

Coward, R. (1985). *Female Desire: Women's Sexuality Today*. London: Paladin.

Eagleton, T. (2015). *Hope Without Optimism*. Charlottesville: University of Virginia Press.

Ehrenreich, B. (2009). *Bright Sided: How the Relentless Promotion of Positive Thinking Has Undermined America*. New York: Metropolitan Books.

Festinger, L. (2009 [1956]). *When Prophesy Fails*. London: Pinter and Martin.

Foer, F. (2019, September 20). Greta Thunberg Is Right to Panic. *The Atlantic Monthly*. Retrieved on March 21, 2020 from https://www.theatlantic.com/ideas/archive/2019/09/greta-thunbergs-despair-is-entirely-warranted/598 492/.

Foucault, M. (1991). Governmentality (R. Braidotti, Trans., and revised by Colin Gordon, in G. Burchell, C. Gordon and P. Miller [Eds.]), *The Foucault Effect: Studies in Governmentality* (pp. 87–104). Chicago, IL: University of Chicago Press.

Good, M.-J. D., Good, B., Schaefer, C., & Lind, S. E. (1990). American Oncology and the Discourse on Hope. *Culture, Medicine and Psychiatry, 14*(1), 59–79.

Jenkins, T. (2013). *Of Flying Saucers and Social Scientists: A Re-reading of When Prophesy Fails and of Cognitive Dissonance*. New York: Palgrave MacMillan.

Jütten, T. (2019). Adorno on Hope. *Philosophy and Social Criticism, 45*(3), 284–306.

Kübler Ross, E. (2009 [1973]). *On Death and Dying*. London: Routledge.

Lear, J. (2006). *Radical Hope: Ethics in the Face of Cultural Devastation*. Cambridge, MA: Harvard University Press.

Levitas, R. (2010 [1990]). *The Concept of Utopia*. Oxford: Peter Lang.

Moreira, T., & Palladino, P. (2005). Between Truth and Hope: On Parkinson's Disease, Eurotransplantation and the Production of the 'Self'. *History of the Human Sciences, 18*, 55–82.

Morgan, M. (2016). The responsibility for social hope. *Thesis Eleven, 136*(1), 107–123.

Nietzsche, F. (1984). *Human, All Too Human*. London: Penguin Books.

Novas, C. (2006). The Political Economy of Hope: Patients' Organizations, Science and Biovalue. *BioSocieties, 1*(3), 289–305.

Petersen, A. (2015). *Hope in Health: The Socio-Politics of Optimism*. Basingstoke: Palgrave Macmillan.

Reed, I. (2007). Why Salem Made Sense: Culture, Gender, and the Puritan Persecution of Witchcraft. *Cultural Sociology, 1*(2), 209–234.

Rose, N. (2007). *The Politics of Life Itself: Biomedicine, Power, and Subjectivity in the Twenty-First Century*. Princeton, NJ: Princeton University Press.

Rose, N., & Novas, C. (2005). Biological Citizenship. In A. Ong & S. Collier (Eds.), *Global Assemblages: Technology, Politics and Ethics as Anthropological Problems* (pp. 439–463). Malden, MA: Blackwell.

Sharp, G. (1973). *The Politics o Nonviolent Action*. Boston, MA: Porter Sargent Publishers.

Terpe, S. (2014). Negative Hopes: Social Dynamics of Isolating and Passive Forms of Hope. *Sociological Research Online*. Retrieved on March 25, 2020 from https://journals.sagepub.com/doi/full/10.5153/sro.3799?casa_token= ppAC6_V2nkAAAAA%3AIlDeGczr7_6ciZfSMkxpdPU1agACHQHf0L XN62fHgkO1UH0riejmkix_K6RajJfjd2XryyxUVyE.

Weber, M. (2011). *The Protestant Ethic and the Spirit of Capitalism*. Oxford: Oxford University Press.

2

Carrying the Dream

In what became, probably, his most famous speech (his address to the March on Washington for Jobs and Freedom on August 28, 1963 at the Lincoln Memorial, Washington, D.C.), Martin Luther King Junior spoke of how he had, 'a dream'. Hope's dream is always about a better tomorrow and whether for an individual, family, nation, or the world, hope is the dream that—someday—that better world will happen.

The most famous poem in Norway, Olav H. Hauge's *It is the dream* (*Det er den draumen* [2019]), speaks of how the writer hopes that everything—the heart, the mountain, the springs—will 'open up' and with it, the dream will 'open up' so that, 'one day' we may glide in upon a little bay we 'never knew was there'. It is important, this imagery of opening, of dreaming, and of the mountain, and it will recur as I develop the argument throughout these chapters.

Some have suggested that hoping and dreaming are distinct activities, with hopes understood as 'within the realm of the possible' (Nilsen 1999: 179), and dreams located 'out of time and out of personal space' (Nilsen 1999: 190). In this conception, dreams, 'cannot be related to in a "rational" manner' (Nilsen 1999: 181).

T. DeNora, *Hope*, https://doi.org/10.1007/978-3-030-69870-6_2

Along these lines, some have criticized hope because for turning us away from the present and the practical. But hope, as sociologist Les Back once put it, is also, 'an attention to the present and the expectation that something will happen that will be unexpected and this will gift an unforeseen opportunity' (Back 2015: n.p.). The poetic language Back uses to describes this attention itself exemplifies the importance of dreaming, or poetic thinking, to the more practical (and perhaps also 'rational' in a richer sense of that word) effort of hoping and taking action for change, and I shall develop this theme more fully in Chapter 5. Back speaks of, 'an attentiveness to the moments when "islands of hope" are established and the social conditions that makes their emergence possible' (ibid.). This concern—with 'islands of hope', understood as a focus on hope as activity, more specifically as the activity of carrying a dream, is the focus of this chapter. I will not agree that dreaming is irrational or, rather, that the irrational cannot be a source of knowledge, and a source of change. This idea has, of course, been at the heart of much philosophical work devoted to utopian thought, nowhere more prominently than in Ernst Bloch's major works, *Spirit of Utopia* (2000) and *Principle of Hope* (1986). And so, we need to return again to Bloch and his abiding concern with hope, and in particular now, with dreaming, understood, I suggest, as a component of hope-as-action.

2.1   Dreaming and Hoping

Bloch champions the imagination and dreaming (day-dreaming) as a key feature in effecting change and as an example of activity that exemplifies human volition. 'The day-dream,' he says, 'is formed consciously. It is "within our power". The day-dream runs the spectrum from silly and escapist to shaped art' (1986: 87–88, quoted in Brown 2003: n.p.). For Bloch, and in relation to utopian visions, hope is 'the waking dream' (2000: n.p.). As Judith Brown (2003: n.p.) puts it, imagination, 'is the fulcrum round which "dreams and life" come to have a realistic relationship to one another." In her sociological study of utopian thought, Ruth Levitas speaks also of how important 'fantasy, imagination, and art' are, 'in sustaining and ultimately realizing an alternative way of being' (Levitas 1990: 164).

As will be developed in some detail in Chapter 5, I see dreaming as part of what the sociologist Paul Atkinson speaks of as 'the artfulness of everyday action' (Atkinson 2020: 168). Dreaming is part of hope's magical realism, a form of 'subtle consciousness', in Even Thompson's term (2017: 6). To hope, I suggest, is to inhabit 'phenomenal' consciousness (as opposed to access consciousness) (Thompson 2017: 8), that is, to hope is to inhabit a realm somewhere in between being fully anaesthetised (and 'unconscious') and fully awake and alert and focused on 'the here and now'. To dream, as Thompson has described (2017: 4) it, is to inhabit a kind of liminal state in which we take materials from the world (the waking, or 'real' world and the 'other' world), break them down and rearrange them and so making a different world. Ultimately, I see that the acknowledgement of dreaming as a valid form of orientation to the present is about open-access to reality's representation. It is a way of acknowledging alternate visions and thus a way of enriching our understanding of the present, its parameters and possibilities. How the borderland between fantasy and reality comes to be defined and reinforced is, in other words, distinctly political, with a small p and a capital P and I have described this politics in previous work (DeNora 2014). This matter is critical when we consider what it might mean to speak of hope and inequality—for example feminist hope, or 'demented' hope matters with which I address more carefully in Chapter 5 ('Who can hope').

2.2   Defining Hope

Thus, dreaming is integral, and necessary, to hoping and in what follows, I shall define hoping with the words from the title of Olav H. Hauge's poem, *The Dream We Carry* (Hauge 2019). Hope is the form of activity that *carries* (*ber*, in Nynorsk; bærer in Bokmål) or *bears* a dream.

This is an idea shared by many others and in many contexts, most famously, as already considered, by Dr Martin Luther King. More recently, and in light of the Black Lives Matters movement, it has been developed by the activist-writer, DeRay McKesson who, in distinguishing hope from faith says, 'faith is rooted in certainty; hope in possibility and they both require their own different kinds of work' (McKesson 2017: 6). McKesson goes on to suggest that we:

> Consider the notion of "hope" in relation to that of "dream" – a word with a similar dual use. On the one hand, a dream can be the fanciful whimsy of a child, free to explore any one of countless possible realities, completely unmoored from present-day circumstance. But dreams have another, more actionable meaning. Indeed, they can be a firm, dynamic vision of where you want to go. I think this is why we still celebrate the dream of Dr. King and why parents urge their kids to dream. (McKesson 2017: 7–8)

To this end, we need to explore in some detail the 'work' of hope and what 'having hope' may do for us, how it may be linked, for example, to wellbeing. In what follows, I shall suggest that wellbeing be understood as a prerequisite for action—that it involves being fit—and energised—for action, being motivationally strong. For this reason, I will devote a chapter to the topic of hope and health, from within a critical, cultural sociological framework. This framework views physical and embodied conditions as connected to social and cultural milieus or as I prefer, ecologies. We need to examine closely the psychological and social dynamics of what it means to speak of hope as work and the cultural resources that fuel hope's work and vision. And that means we need to consider how dreams work and what dreaming does in relation to 'reality'. But first, what does it mean to speak of 'carrying' a dream?

2.3   Defining 'to Carry'

The term 'carry' is laden with multiple meanings and in what follows I consider some of these in order to develop a schema (by no means definitive—it is heuristic, designed to prompt further thinking and research). So, to 'carry' can mean to *bring* something with us, so as to keep it close as we move through time and space. In this sense, we are bearing a load.

You might, for example, carry me if I could not swim and we needed to cross a river. That carrying a load in turn implies a second meaning of the term—commitment and value, a *protective* (conservationist) attitude toward what is carried—you value, perhaps, me, or you value being able to give help to others and seek to protect that value, keep it secure—you seek to maintain the dream and its accoutrements, the things you carry.

But to carry can also mean, third, to *project*, as when our voices carry across a distance. If you project your voice across the river, perhaps to encourage others also to swim across, and you say, 'I know we will get there safely', you are placing a hope (stated as a probable outcome) audibly in space. By speaking (and this is central to all that follows), you have changed the acoustical composition of that space (for example it was quiet and now there is a voice) and you have changed the emotional tension of that space (you have inflected it with your confidence—projecting a hope in the form of a confidence that hope will be realised). Thus, we can speak of carrying (a dream) as involving a kind of projection of a dream into space, physically, as when we are audible, or visibly, as when physically enacting or pursuing dreams, but also symbolically, as when we bring meaningful materials conducive to a dream into a physical space, or into the social/psychological space that is consciousness.

The sense of something being carried across time and space points to a fourth understanding of what it means to carry or be carried, namely, *infecting*. Social scientists often speak of cultural contagion. That refers to how things are carried, or projected, over time and space in ways that are 'caught' and spread (and in a post-Covid 19 universe we are all too familiar with the negative connotations of contagion). There are times when contagion is to be desired. For example, to pursue the example of crossing a river, I might hope to catch your courage and conviction that we will travel safely across and if I do, my hope is strengthened and renewed and so am I—I have more strength now to bear, or carry on with, what I must or need to do, despite the risk. So too, we can 'catch' moods, practices, values, stylistic patterns of behavior, and beliefs. (Indeed, we can 'catch' them so much sometimes that we become, 'carried away'.) In this sense 'carrying' hope is, potentially 'infecting' others with hope, or 'catching' what is 'carried' by others. And just as with disease, infection can be described in terms of its mechanisms, the conditions under which things are more or less likely to 'catch on' or become contagious.

Finally, fifth, we often speak of something being carried in the sense that it comes to be it is *realised* or fulfilled, brought into being—a motion in a meeting was carried, for example. As we will see, what counts as the realisation of a dream is always a matter for negotiation. We constantly adapt our dreams since dreams and circumstances of dreaming are always in flux. Our dreams undergo metamorphosis according to what, as our circumstances change, we are physically, psycho-socially, able to carry. Moreover, in some circumstances hope's realisation may be less important than hope as an activity and this theme will be explored in Chapter 5.

Hope, then, can be thought of as a form of locally produced activity—and thinking of hope in this way calls attention to what Fine (2012: 1) describes as 'tiny publics' where 'the power of immediate surroundings and microcultures', too often overlooked in favour of 'large-scale' forces, can contribute enormously to change. It is for this reason that I have suggested that hope should be understood as activity, and that as an activity, hope is multi-faceted, composed of the five interrelated forms of carrying a dream: bringing, protecting, projecting, infecting, and realizing. Each of these facets (and we could no doubt enumerate more of them—I make no claim to having produced an exhaustive list) highlights what it is we do when we hope. They are worth now exploring now in greater detail since, as a kind of heuristic schema, they provide the conceptual backdrop for the chapters that follow.

2.4   Bringing

If carrying a dream involves bringing, and thus, keeping near to us the thing or things we hope for, then we need to examine just what it is that we might be carrying, in this sense. These things can be material objects that we keep physically close to us when we are on the move, things that, when we are 'in transition' can offer symbols, emblems and reminders of our hopes. 'Things' are often of vital importance—the anthropologist

Daniel Miller suggests that 'stuff' can both enhance and suppress aspects of who we are and what we can be (Miller 2010).

Think of a student, off to university for the first time. She or he may bring photos from happy times or important occasions, or a poster for the dormitory wall that signals affiliation, aspiration or identity For example, I remember when I went off to West Chester to study music I brought what I considered to be a very sophisticated, very large poster I had purchased at the G. Schirmer music store in New York City circa 1975, which featured a cartoon portrait of a perplexed or bemused-looking Ludwig van Beethoven with a naked, sackbut-playing, cello-hugging, long-haired woman caught in his tangled hair, drawn by the German cartoonist and illustrator Michael Mathias Prechtl. It had the caption, 'Beethoven is alive and living at G Schirmer' [Prechtl 1974]. I had no idea at that time that I would later write a PhD thesis and then a book (DeNora 1995) on Beethoven. It might seem simply fey to suggest that my poster 'knew' or 'presaged' something that I only became aware of down the line (though I kept that poster well after graduating and its image stayed with me as I embarked upon postgraduate study) As I will explore presently, what we bring with us, when we cannot bring everything, has a great deal to do with what and how and why we project our dreams and demonstrate them to others and ourselves.

Now, by contrast, think of people who make arduous journeys in search of asylum or a better life. In 2014 and 2015 UK newspapers were full of stories with titles such as, 'What do Refugees Bring With Them' or 'What is in a Refugee's Bag'? One of these was a photo essay for *Time Magazine* by James Mollison and Megan Gibson in 2015 (Mollison and Gibson 2015). The authors interviewed refugees at a refugee stop in Nicklesdorf, Austria. Each person was asked if they would allow Mollison to make a portrait photograph of them along with their most precious possession(s), the things they had chosen to hold on to during their perilous journeys:

> Some people we met were even eager to show us what they carried: cell phones or digital cameras with photos of loved ones who they had been separated from during the journey. These devices, and the photos on

them, held their greatest hopes of being reunited with a missing mother, a lost son or a wife, two-months pregnant and nowhere to be found.

Others, for example Parastoo, a 23-year-old mother who travelled with her husband and young child described how a pendant was precious because she associated it with the aspirations for their journey:

> I bought this pendant a year ago in Iran. It has part of the Quran written on paper inside it. I wear it to bring us luck. It worked – we're here. (Mollison and Gibson 2015)

It is easy to see how objects fulfill different functions for those who hope and how the 'bringing' of objects is part of hope understood as an activity. Objects are talismans and charms for the future, as described by Parastoo. They are reminders of what one hopes for (photographs of loved ones with whom one hopes to be someday reunited). Objects stand in as emblems of what is hoped for and as such they may serve as part of people's everyday rituals, and planned, future ritual scenarios, linked to hope.

For example, a Unicef study, 'Hope in their hands: Refugee children share their keepsakes' describes what children bring with them when they flee their homes and the reasons for their choices, often chosen because they are associated with happy memories or because they make the child feel safe, but sometimes because they are part of what is carried as a hope:

> Yara, 10, holds her doll, a birthday gift from her father. She has named the doll Farah. "It got scary in Syria. There were shootings. Dad said get your stuff together, we're going," she says. "I wanted to bring [my] teddy bear, but my parents said no, it was too big, so I put Farah in my bag." Yara wants to return to Syria someday, and has pledged to bring Farah back with her. "I will dress her up and get her ready and we will go. But this time, I'm bringing all of my toys."
>
> Rudaina, 11, still has her house keys from Syria. "I brought them with me because when we go back to Syria, I'm going to be the one who opens the door," she says. Rudaina, who is in the fourth grade at a school in the Za'atari camp, doesn't remember her native country, but says that her parents told her it was beautiful. "We once had a home, but now we live

in a caravan. I feel so sad when I hold the keys because I'm so far away from home," she says. (Herwig and Brune 2019)

*   *   *

The plight of displaced people, migrants, and refugees, perhaps most starkly highlights how people, 'on the move' carry or bring with them things that keep hope alive. That carrying of objects, understood as 'technologies of memory' is a way of holding on to the sense of, 'who one is, where one has been, and where one is headed' (Güran-Aydin and DeNora 2016: 233). In less traumatic lives, we find similar examples since 'displacement' is likely to affect all of us—eventually—as we become infirm, and likely to affect some of us—at any time—if we encounter adverse circumstances. What might we (be able to) 'carry' if or when we need to enter a homeless shelter, hospital, or prison? What will we bring when we enter a care home or hospice? And how might those objects reflect, but also shape, the ways we hope, and our understandings of what it might be appropriate or realistic to hope for (we return to this topic in Chapter 3)?

Consider my own Great Aunt Elsie: trained as a nurse in the 1920s, married to a chemist, and living in the same small house for fifty years. She and her husband gardened enthusiastically (competing fiercely in annual dahlia growers' competitions). She was, as people used to say, deft with a needle. They were keen bird-watchers. As a child, I was intrigued by their home which was full of curiosities, some of which came from Elsie's childhood home in Southampton, Long Island—a needlepoint fire screen, hand crocheted lace antimacassars on the armchairs, crewelwork tablecloths, a mercury glass butler's ball, twin glass vases over the fireplace filled with seashells (collected on her and her husband's honeymoon on Sanibel Island), gooseneck lamps, books, plants, amateur artworks painted by a friend, myriad photographs in polished frames, china collections from her great grandparents, a cabinet full of antique glassware…

Two years after her husband died, Elsie, then in her late 80s, fell and broke a hip. Although she eventually regained some mobility, she was no longer able to live at home. In consultation with her niece (she had no children), she eventually decided to enter a small care home not far from her former family home. This decision led to the sale of her family home and most of its contents. That meant Elsie needed not only to think about what she hoped for during what were clearly her final years of life 'in care' but, more immediately, which objects she wished to retain. She chose a bright painting of flowers created by best friend (which after she died hung on my mother's bedroom wall and now hangs in my home—would I 'bring' it with me if or when I move to a care facility I wonder?), a hand-crocheted throw that she had made and which used to be at the foot of her bed, some family photographs, a small decorative table, a handmade doily, and a few special pieces of jewelry (including her wedding ring) that held sentimental value.

These things that she 'carried' were more than reminders of her previous way of life. Though they were not, as in the examples considered earlier, talismans keeping her hopeful of a return to a previous life; rather, they were more like allies assisting transition and helping her to retain a modified hope, one that consisted, as she said at the time, of the hope of making the best of things in reduced circumstances. These things were also allies in the sense that they helped her to remember her life and late husband, her former friends, which was part of a larger project of sustaining meaning and memory until the end (which she managed until her death at age 92). And they, very simply, were things that gave her pleasure, that she liked. Elsie's hope, one might conjecture, was to not forget and, ultimately, for the things she valued not to be forgotten. So too, consider Serena, a resident in a care home (she has since died):

Serena [is] distressed in a way I've seen before when she's thrown by circumstances or something happening, then gets into anxiety about her end of life situation. She's clutching a letter from the hospital asking to come in for more scans. She doesn't want to know about this, says "No operations at [my age]!". But it brings the situation into relief for her, and she's fretting again about what she will leave behind— primarily the canary [she has been allowed to keep her pet bird in the care home]! But then she calms down and gets into the usual narrative mode with me, and other things come up that are linked to this. How her solicitor she says will make sure that her treasured possessions boxed in the wardrobe will be treated properly after she's gone. She holds up a few things that she loves, ornaments on the side of the dressing table–a porcelain ashtray with a sentimental [illustration]. She tells me an involved story about this, and also about other similar pieces from the collection of figurines. They were brought in Harrods with her mother in the 1940s or 50s, figures of dolls and angels ..

These are the things she loves, and the detailed descriptions are the signs of this love– what they are aesthetically, but also what they conjure up in memory, how they link to people, to her past life. The conversation moves to what we love– who, what– people, things.... (Ansdell, Reflections on Care for Music)

* * *

Though Elsie's and Serena's circumstances and opportunities were highly constrained, both found ways to continue to exert some power of choice (the things they brought) which in turn empowered their ability to live in new circumstances, furnishing their living spaces with significant things, and enabling them to hope, realistically, including hoping that someone would come to cherish their things after they were gone. Not everyone who moves into a care home has such agency and there are times when the things that we bring are chosen on our behalf. When a loved one living with dementia moves to a care home, a family may have to decide 'what she/he would have chosen'. In such a situation, it is possible to see a kind of hoping on behalf for that person ('She would have hoped to have this figurine'). In these cases, we are helping another to carry things because of *our* hopes for them and thus for us ('this is what father would have wanted with him'). These situations also highlight how the things that people choose to carry, or the things people choose for people to carry, and to hope for (and vicariously hope for), are part of a relational matrix of shared, and sometimes conflicted, aspirations.

* * *

So far, the concept of movement has been considered in terms of physical movement (such as relocation or migration), and the concept of carrying, in terms of physical objects. But there are other types of movement, and other types of objects to be carried. Taking objects first, much of what we, individually and/or collectively, 'bring with us' when on the move is symbolic and cognitive, and much of it involves remembering, bringing or carrying memories with us as part of hope's springboard.

Memories linked to hopes are carried by individuals and groups moving through space and time on a daily basis. In a phenomenological study of remembering, Edward Casey (2000) describes how memories are carried through reminiscing and how that process may proceed in different ways. Reminiscing may involve individual 'musing' on the past in a free-form manner but it may also be provoked by something one encounters, that provides, as he puts it, 'memorial support'. This support in turn may structure future action trajectories and motivations.

Casey gives the example of coming across old family documents which led to a train of reminiscing (memory work) about a departed relative. This led in turn to the motivation to delve more deeply into that relative's history, which led a return to the papers, which led to further reminiscing (this is what I did in the passages above, when remembering Aunt Elsie— memory being in part 'triggered' by a photograph and a picture). Casey gives a special term to material that help us reminisce—'*reminiscenta*', or, 'anything that survives the epoch being reminisced about' (Casey 2000: 110). So too, I may 'see' my dream, or am put back in contact with my dream, each time I look at a photograph, hear this music (or replay it in my mind) or touch this little object—a pebble, a nut, a charm, or an icon. These things 'put me in mind' again of my dream and help me to 'hold on' to it. For this reason, I might wish to carry these *reminiscenta* with me wherever I go, cherishing and 'protecting' them.

Of course, memories can be triggered by many other things that we do not carry but encounter as object synchronous with the times that we remember. One might be walking through a garden where the smell of a flower triggers memories of a longed-for time, person, place or situation.

But it is often that we carry memories only as memories, that is memories that are not prompted by remnants, *reminiscenta* or other artifacts but rather which we ourselves conjure up as recalled images, fragments of events or experiences, thoughts or sensations. We do this as part of reverie and often in ways that we hope will activate our minds/bodies, eliciting emotion and thought, and perhaps kindling hope for something in the future. These memories are perhaps the most portable of all of the things that we 'carry' or 'bring' with us as we move. During the Bosnian War a visiting colleague from Sarajevo was describing how she had enjoyed a very happy childhood. Talk moved on to the devastation of her home city. She said then something like, 'those happy memories of my childhood are mine and they can never be taken away'. At times, memory provides a refuge and this theme will be explored more fully in Chapter 4.

We 'bring' things with us when we are on the move, things that are physical and things that are part of memory and imagination. And just as these things can be physical or part of our psyche, so too the notion of 'being on the move' can be physical or phenomenological, that is involving a kind of psychological sense of moving. That movement may involve temporal shifts of the psyche, changes in mood and energy levels, motivations and feelings in micro and longer-range time periods. These kinds of movement are affected by the things that we carry and protect. They will in tur affect the quality and intensity of our hope and our capacity for hope. There will be times, for example, when we have a sense that we are 'moving fast' toward a hoped-for goal. There may be hopeful 'moments' (Petersen 2015: 149) where we have fleeting glimpses of better futures ('islands of hope' in Back's words quoted in Chapter 2). And there may be times when despondency strikes, when we are exhausted, when time slows and we feel like 'letting go' of the things we carry which may feel literally or figuratively at those times too heavy to bear or even care about.

Thus, the first sense of hoping, understood as carrying a dream involves bringing things—real or symbolic—with us and bearing their load (physical and/or psychological) as we move through real or psychic spaces over time. We are willing to carry these things, to bear the load, because, of course these things are of very great value to us and because we cannot bear to let them go, because we feel a need to protect them.

2.5   Protecting

If you decide to pack a doll when you flee your homeland so as to stay connected to things that matter to you, you are also displaying a value commitment—to the doll, of course, but also to what it connotes (home, loved ones). The act of keeping it with you (carrying it) shows that you value your attachment to it, that you do not want to be detached from it and that you are willing to go to some trouble to protect it (protect it, value it, care for it). In that act of protecting, you are also enacting a form of hopefulness, namely, you hope to retain, perhaps eventually regain, contact with those and that which you have left behind. In this sense, the role of hope as a moral project is underlined. As the sociologist Sylvia Terpe puts it, with reference to Hans Joas', *The Genesis of Values* (2000), on values and social action:

> … images of a better future signify values, they 'do not [just] express desires, but instead imply what is worth desiring' (Joas 2000: 17). Accordingly, what is expressed in these visions and experiences of hope is regarded as valuable because hope bestows life with (moral) meaning. (Terpe 2014: 2)

These attachments not only articulate our moral compass; they create ourselves and our identities. We—our being and our opportunities for thought and action—are constituted through the network of objects and ideas that are within our reach, literally and figuratively. In this sense too, they constitute our fundamental psychic, and indeed, physical, stability and we will explore this point in the next chapter. In relation to psychic stability (the sense of who we are what in what we believe) the metaphor of hope as an anchor is illuminated—this value-commitment that hope both facilitates and is a function of is what allows us to feel whole, connected, directed and focused as we navigate through, in whatever ways, the unsettled conditions of our life course. So, to hope is to retain a commitment to what we value and in that sense, as discussed before, hope is noble because hope is an ethical activity.

2.6   Bringing with and Protecting

There is an additional and critical aspect of remembering in relation to hope. Often when we hope we are hoping to transcend a difficult past to move into a better future. In relation to that past, the shape of memory can be key to the possibility of transcendence. When memories of trauma (large displacement of people, war, terror) are involved, this question of memory's shape can become urgent and the stakes around how memories take shape are high and the path to what is remembered can be highly dangerous. This is because memories are selective; they are formed in relation to what the sociologist Anna Lisa Tota calls 'technologies of memory' (Tota 2001, 2005) by which she means media—aesthetic and material forms that mediate and formulate memory, structuring perception of the past in ways that enhance some features and suppress others. What is remembered, in other words, is culturally arranged and that arrangement can both facilitate and constrain the pathways to which remembering can take us.

Tota has examined this issue closely through studies of commemoration of terrorist events, specifically following how the cultural forms employed for commemoration are fraught and yet constitute what comes to count as the reality of what is being mourned, held fast, remembered. The ways that commemoration rituals are negotiated inevitably selects, condenses and traduces the lived experience of what occurred and thus is inevitably politicised. Moreover, depending on how commemorations are configured, possibilities for the future—realising change and healing—will be constrained (Tota 2004, 2005). As Tota puts it:

> One of the most effective ways of understanding the social nature of remembering and forgetting as a process is to analyse how it is objectivized, how it takes shape in cultural objects/artefacts. The concept of commemorative genre takes this a step further. A genre is established through a process of canonization, can be of a literary, artistic, musical and even commemorative nature, and can obviously occur in very different ways and with very different characteristics. The creation of a specific genre of remembrance implies the establishment of a series of social conventions which fix what is appropriate and what is not when

representing a given past (from war victims to victims of terrorism, from the victims of the holocaust to those of the mafia, from the victims of road accidents to those of plane accidents). I do not wish by any means to suggest that commemoration of different events *necessarily* implies the consolidation of different commemorative genres (or vice versa of very similar ones). Rather it should be analysed how different institutional contexts have helped define the extent of the variations possible within a given commemorative ritual action. (2004: 139–140)

Remembering is, in other words, inevitably cultural, and the cultural shape and politics of what is, and what is allowed to be, remembered will affect what is even thinkable when contemplating the future—in light of the horizons of what counts as 'real' in the present and the past. The connections, as we shall see, between trauma, whether individual or cultural, and hope involve not only carrying memory but negotiating the tensions around what is to count as shared memory. (For example, a photograph or a poem features some aspects of the past and can therefore draw attention toward those, away from others. It will 'cast' or 'fix' the past into forms that filter the wider and more complex set of what might have been remembered. So, memory is perhaps more like a work of art, a composition and less like a panoramic record of 'everything' that happened.)

If memory, whether individual or collective, is understood as culturally mediated, that is, taking shape in relation to the cultural materials that affect how one remembers, then the social relations of what we carry as remembrances is a central part of the study of hope, hope's genesis and development. Tota's work, in company with a number of key scholars has been in the forefront of an area of study addressed to 'cultural trauma'. The focus on cultural trauma is devoted to the collective interpreted experiences of horrendous events—violence, atrocity, terrorism, environmental/social/technological disaster—how these things come to be raised into consciousness and memory, politicized, and reworked over time in relation to cultural media ('technologies') and rituals. The shape of these forms and rituals is central to processes, and even the possibility of, recovery, reparation, and justice. As Ron Eyerman puts it, cultural trauma is an occurrence that not only:

"tears the social fabric," but also that this tear must be (1) articulated and represented, (2) "laden with negative affect," and (3) accepted by a group. (2019: 5)

Eyerman describes how the articulation (projection) of a cultural trauma will include:

> meaning struggle, a process involving competing interpretations of what precisely has occurred, who was responsible, and what should be done to repair the tear (2019: 5)

How traumatic memories are used is part of the study of cultural trauma. As is how they are managed and connected to other things that are carried within projects of hoping. In a study of Holocaust survivors in occupied Germany, Mankowitz (2002) describes how part of the process of moving into a hoped-for future involved, and was championed by certain religious leaders, a situation in which young people should, 'create and build, and dance, and sing' so that this resurgence of life in the aftermath of trauma would serve as an appropriate 'revenge' (Mankowitz 2002: 81). Here, it is possible to see how hoping for the future may involve a careful management of collective memory (what one 'carries', 'protects' and 'projects'). In the case described by Mankowitz, memory of atrocity is galvanised as a means for driving life forward. Here, memory is re-charged in ways that project a culture of hope for the future. Mankowitz describes how trauma memories were deliberately woven into speeches at forward-looking, festive occasions such as wedding receptions (Mankowitz: 222).

Drawing on Eyerman, and Tota, I suggest that how we represent and remember, how we draw on shared cultural representations of past events, provides preconditions for how we are able to hope. And here, emotion plays an important role in the representation of past trauma, as Eyerman describes:

> I note that all references to "trauma" entail a strong emotional affect; in effect, I am asking, why employ the term if one seeks to avoid this connotation? I argue that the idea of a specifically "cultural" trauma should embrace rather than abandon this emotional dimension, regardless of

whether the root cause of the emotion is "real," (i.e., stemming from something that has actually occurred), or imagined. Of course, such reactions *are* real for those who believe an incident to be real… It is not necessary that such an event actually occurred so long as it "is believed to undermine" a culture or a collective identity. The powerful emotions this belief evokes are real in either case… (2019: 10)

As with trauma, so too hope in the aftermath of trauma may arise in response to things that are felt, and thus that are 'real'. We turn to the future, the dream or vision, and seek to 'bear' it precisely when we cannot or will not 'bear' the present. And the shape of memory in turn shapes how we understand both present and future; it is culturally mediated. At times that mediation can be quite strategically or therapeutically composed (as in the example from Mankowitz where traumatic memories were harnessed to an affirming dream of future flourishing), and this issue will be explored in Chapter 4. The interrelationship between remembering and representation, remembering and hoping, whether hoping for restoration of a previous time, relationship or situation, or for restitution after trauma, is an active ingredient of hoping. Memory—mediated, negotiated, potentially fraught, dangerous—is thus one of the most important things that we carry (bring and protect) when we carry a dream. How we let those things that we bring and protect 'carry' within a space (mental, symbolic or physical) is the next feature of how a dream is carried—'projection'.

2.7   Projecting

To hope, then, is to be able to carry and protect dreams, dreams that we are committed to in moral terms. I began this book by considering the various critiques of hope and in particular the critique that hope was 'passive', something antithetical to action. At the end of that discussion I suggested that too much about hope and what it does is overlooked if we discussions of hope are overly general. I suggested that what is required instead is a consideration of hoping as an activity, and through specific case-study examples of hope as it is enacted. Perhaps the right place to begin thinking about whether hope can be part of activism, part of action for change, is to think yet more closely about this third sense of what it means to bring or carry something which involves thinking about how hope itself 'carries' or can be carried, or projected, between people and in, and across, space and time.

Projection is central to what it means to carry a dream: and considering projection begins to underline the importance of cultural materials and cultural practice to the activity of hoping. I use this term in a sense that differs markedly from its psychoanalytic connotations. There, projection is about how we offload on to others things that we cannot handle or process ourselves, as when, for example, we shift and reallocate blame, directing it away from ourselves. By contrast, I understand projection here to consist of a developing and elaborating a dream through shared through words and imagery, knowledge, customs, sensory patterns such as smells and tastes, rhythms and tones. Projection, then, helps to 'carry' the dream by allowing that dream to infiltrate consciousness and lived present experience.

By this logic, to project something into a space is to furnish space and to furnish is to make a change. That change may take place in only in my consciousness—for example I remember an event or person or material in my past. Let's say, it might include a memory of what I did on All Souls Day in a particular year (visited a church in London and walked through a garden), or a memory of a loved one (living or dead), or a room (in a building or a museum or my old family home)—by remembering these things I can furnish my present consciousness, divert my thoughts from something else, and 'inhabit' the space I have just created—in my head. Similarly, projection may take place outside my consciousness, in my physical and social surroundings—I place an object here or there and it helps to, as it were, 'keep me or us in mind' of the things that I am hoping (every time I look across the room, for example, at that painting or vase, or hold this stone in my hand, I remember…).

In both of these examples of projecting, the cultural activity of putting something into space, no matter how small a thing, whether mental or physical, is also a form of cultural activism; it carries things into a space in ways that reconfigure that space as a space that is future-oriented. This is carrying a dream in the sense of allowing parts of the dream to occupy space and so at least symbolically, through a process of synecdoche or allowing a part of the dream to stand on behalf of the whole, to change that space. As we will see in Chapter 5, this change, if it transpires in shared or public space, can provide an opportunity for cultural activism and thus for realising a dream insofar as the space is incrementally filled, little by little, with aspects of a dream. Projecting is in other words critical to a dream's retention and critical to the collective carrying of a dream over time/space.

The cultural sociologist Robert W. Witkin speaks of what he called, 'holding forms', or:

> …the seed of which the full expressive form is the flower…the kernel of inspiration…motif…to encapsulate only the essential movement of the sensate impulse and to hold that movement in consciousness for the duration of the expressive act…the oak in the acorn…any expressive medium can be used to make a holding form. A sequence of gestures, a certain rhythm or pitch sequence…. (1974: 181)

We might say, then, that projecting things into a space (letting them 'carry') is the activity of furnishing space with forms capable of holding our hope, and therefore, stabilizing a dream. If hope is an anchor, it is itself anchored by cultural materials and cultural practices the genesis and development of which itself deserves close scrutiny and that is the topic of Chapter 4. So, projecting involves an attempt to furnish the spaces within which we live, move, think, feel and act with materials that hold things for us and that help us, in Back's sense, to hold an, 'attention to the present'. This holding is part of what keeps us motivated and focused on the dream until such time as it can or might unfold, or while it is unfolding. To project a dream in other words is to create a space that contains resources that can be used to call our attention to potentialities, opportunities, minute changes and signs, and to incipience: the project, then, is to cultivate our lived environments so that they are conducive to growing dreams and that is in turn to contribute to changing that environment and what it will support.

* * *

2.8 Private Projection

In the activity of projecting, hoping 'carries'; it expands in a space and can extend across groups and across time and space. Even in the act of secret hoping, even if we are unable to share our hopes with anyone, we are engaged in a kind of elaboration and projection of an imagined, and therefore different, world. In the case of hoping in secret—we fill or furnish *mental* space, that is, our consciousness. And even this very private form of projecting can generate possibilities for action. It is therefore worth considering how projecting hope, whether secret hope, shared, public, voiced hope, or something in between, can be understood as part of the activity of building worlds—conceptually, symbolically, imaginatively and socially.

In extreme cases, where people are being held in enforced confinement, or where they are confined in identities or social roles from which they feel there is 'no escape', there is scope for projection. Furnishing mental space by projecting ideas, images or imagined scenarios there does make a change—it changes consciousness, or rather holds consciousness in particular configurations that deflect awareness from the things that would otherwise intensify despondency.

Brian Keenan, who was held as a hostage for over four years in Beirut during the 1980s, describes how, when his guards allowed him to use a shower, he deliberately took as long as he could, so that, if a way out through the shower room were to be found, the guards would assume that he was still showering, allowing time enough:

> to climb the piping and slither like one of those cockroaches through the opening. But it would have to wait. I was still trying to convince myself that I would soon be released. There was no point in pre-empting that freedom by making a failed attempt at escape...During those days I sat complementing hopes for release with plans for escape. (1993: 46)

Here, carrying the dream, in this case a dream of freedom from captivity, involves furnishing consciousness with images and metaphors, projecting a vision of what is hoped for onto one's mental space where those furnishings consist of imagined scenarios ('climb the piping'; being, 'like one of those cockroaches' and thus able to 'slither…through the opening'). As Keenen describes this process, it allowed hope to 'complement' more strategic thinking about possible means for escape.

The activity of hoping, understood as 'carrying' therefore contains an important performative feature even when projection has to take place in an entirely private or secretive realm. In allowing our minds to be filled with visions of what might be the probable impossible. Imaginative projection, inwardly, therefore elaborates a mental world of future scenarios, imaginative possibilities for action. In this sense, letting the dream carry involves crafting 'inside one's head' a model future, in, grammatically speaking, the future-perfect tense (something is going to happen but it is not possible to specify the precise moment when this will occur). As such, projecting hope, even only to one's self, is simultaneously furnishing an alternative, imagined world and as such it can make a person feel empowered, more able and ready to act, if, or when, such a moment should arise. Terry Waite, also held captive during the Lebanon hostage crisis describes, similarly, how during his captivity, when he had no pen or paper, he wrote his story in his imagination—it provided a way in which to hold on to, and prepare for, the possibility of eventual release when he would be able to write for real (Waite 1993: xiii). For this reason, hope as projection is—as will be explored in the next chapter—integral to hope as a resource for health promotion and for wellbeing even in extremis.

2.9   Projecting and Infecting

When projection is outward into a social space (symbolic and/or physical, communicative) it can be shared, and when hope carries between people, that resource can be grown (mutual infectiousness). Within the sociology of affect, the study of emotional contagions describes how moods and emotions can be 'caught' (Gibbs 2001), their 'infectiousness' as, through varied mechanisms such as mimicry of facial expressions, embodied stances such as posture, and vocal utterances, feedback to these things, and—according to some accounts—the firing of mirror neurons that produce a sensation or feeling of something that is otherwise only being witnessed (Hatfield et al. 2014). Through this 'interaffectivity', as Daniel Stern describes it (Stern 2018 [1985]), emotions spread, from one to two to whole groups. Emotions and orientations are, in short, infectious. Their contagion involves a kind of affective resonance, or reciprocal modulation between people that consists of a relational process of affecting and being affected (Mühlhoff 2019). And contagion is, as I shall discuss in more detail presently, central to resistance.

In a second book, co-authored with fellow captive John McCarthy, Brian Keenan and McCarthy describe how during their time together, incarcerated in a dungeon, they planned, as the title describes it, 'a journey beyond imagination'. They elaborated plans to walk across Patagonia. This imagined journey allowed them to co-create a vision of what could and would be done 'when' they were released. Their talk about the imagined journey allowed them to inhabit a shared fantasy and to time travel into the future-perfect when it 'would' happen. (The two actually made the journey five years after they were released and the book describes both the imagined journey and the real one in terms of how it squared with its prefiguration during captivity.)

Here, Keenen and McCarthy's shared projection can be said to involve a kind of exponential multiplication of the resources that each of them separately carried and projected. Here, shared fantasy and shared cultural terrain (a space of symbols, images, visions, elaborations of dreams) allowed the dream to become infectious, for a shared culture to develop that strengthened the dream. The social and cultural history of collective movements and collective resistance has long been concerned with 'carriers' and contagion.

In his study of underground culture in the former Czechoslovakia, and building on the work of Even Ruud (2002), Trever Hagen describes how shared cultural, and specifically musical, furnishing of scenes made it possible, as Hagen puts it, to 'connect people together in action and consciousness' (2019: xii) and in ways that could then be converted into, that generated, collective power for activism and 'immunity':

... Ruud (2002, 2008: 48) has described music's health technologies as "cultural immunogens." By this Ruud refers to music as a medium for care of the self—how it can come to regulate emotions, aide in coping,

maintain concentration, and also keep out, or replace, unwanted "pollu-
tants" within an ecology … This type of immunization is… accomplished
and achieved through community activity.

Hagen goes on to describe how 'immunizing' a collective was for the
members of the Underground movement:

> a form of aesthetic resistance to the 'sea of mental poverty' and
> the 'unhealthiness' of normalization conditions linked to 'official
> culture'…[it] occurred in secure spaces that were furnished for habitation
> wherein one could feel certain emotions and adopt subject positions….
> (Hagen 2019: 92)

Hagen speaks of a three-step process involved in connecting people,
action, and consciousness: locating, opening up, and crafting. In the
context of underground culture, that three-step process produced an
alternative, resistant ('habitable') cultural ecology, or way of life, which
took shape through the ways that a 'collective feedback loop' expanded
hopeful visions and tapped resources for the growth of collective hope.
As Hagen understands it, communities, depending upon how they are
created and sustained, promote public wellbeing:

> Such collective immunization highlights two qualities of community:
> *commune* (sharing with) and *immunity* (resistance from). Cohen (1985:
> 15) points out that boundaries may be thrown up and accentuated for
> protection (or prevention) for collective well-being. In a similar fashion
> Derrida has alluded to these forms of exclusion through his alternative
> reading of community: "to have *communion* is to be fortified on all sides,
> to build a "common" (*com*) "defense" (*munis*), as when a wall is put
> up around the city to keep the stranger or foreigner out" (Derrida and
> Caputo 1997: 108 qtd in Ansdell 2004: 80). Or when a boundary is
> assembled to keep out establishments…..In short immunity is implicated
> in coming together (which is in itself a cultural activity of "upkeep") and
> therefore a question of resistance ("keeping out"). (Hagen 2019: 17)

As we will explore in Chapters 3 and 4, the concept of immunity and
'cultural immunogens'—and the idea of deflecting what is detrimental to

health and wellbeing has become central in cross- and inter-disciplinary studies of wellbeing and mental health. These studies in turn have increasingly considered hope's role in relation to immunity and well-being. So, how we heal and how we hope and resist political and cultural forms of 'dis-ease' (Ruud 2002, 2020) are reciprocal and this reciprocity itself is an important topic for research on hope and hoping.

Creating culture together, engaging with ideas, images, media, and being involved in sharing these things, projects hope across spaces, people, and time. Embedding visions and dreams in media that will 'carry' them is part of how hope expands and can be seen to power collective action in the sense of providing materials that structure and undergird mood, emotion, and motivation. In their study of music and social movement activity, Ron Eyermean and Andrew Jameson describe how songs of resistance during the period of slavery in American came to be appropriated (or 'located, opened up and crafted' in Hagen's [2019] terminology) as resources for hope and in ways that came to 'carry' the impulses of the civil rights movement of the mid-twentieth century:

> These songs carried a message of hope and transcendence through the decades of struggle even after formal emancipation. It was these songs which formed the basis for the "freedom" songs which were so important during the civil rights movement in the 1950s and 1960s. (1998: 44)

As Eyerman and Jameson describe, music not only projected the shared, or potentially shared, vision of change, not only held that in a space where it could be then reviewed and where it could fire feeling and moti-vation. The projection of culture, here music, into and across people, time and space could also, at times, prefigure what might happen next, ways of acting/feeling down the line. They quote Tod Gitlin, president of the Students for a Democratic Society (SDS), a key organization in the development of the new left in the 1960s. As they put it, 'Gitlin remem-bers one moment in the early 1960s, the "days of hope" that preceded the "days of rage" at the end of that decade':

> Dylan sang for us…We followed his career as if he were singing our song; we got in the habit of asking where he was taking us next…. (1998: 116)

So, part of what we 'carry' when we hope is cultural material (visions, imagery, media) that depicts, models, mirrors or otherwise represents and holds that hope in ways that furnish our space, mental or physical, isolated or shared, in ways that keep us focused and that motivate us to continue to dream and, through dreaming, engage in imaginative action and thus planning. What is projected outward into space (even into our own private mental space) is in turn available to be 'caught'—in the sense of contagion or infection but also in the sense of catching something that is thrown from one person to another, or which takes root and develops in our consciousness.

For these reasons, social movement theorists have been interested for a long time now in aesthetic media. The question of how movements move and grow is one about cultural creation and dissemination, and cultural contiguity and contagion—how increasing numbers of people can give each other 'the bug' of motivation and how that infection involves coming into contact with infectious media. The concept of 'trend' does not quite capture this process; not only is it an external observation (of something that has happened—a rise or decline in a form of consumption for example—rather than an attempt to under-stand what happened in terms of how that trend began and developed) the concept of trend also does not capture the ways that infection is laden with emotion. 'Catching' motivation, or feeling, involves many things. It involves learning how to desire images, ideas, visions, and becoming 'converted', that is to experiencing perceptual alterations that then charge reality in new ways. This affective dimension to social action is well understood—as the 'hearts and minds' issue—by political campaigners, advertising industries, marketing firms, and charismatic religious leaders. It involves the crafting and prototyping of desire and that topic has been well-addressed in previous studies (Hennion and Méadel 1989; Slaby and von Scheve 2019).

2.10 Realising

At the time that Martin Luther King Jr gave his "I have a dream" speech some activists considered that the speech proved that, 'we had "dreamers" instead of leaders leading us' (Younge 2013: 12). Young suggests that, 'the speech sets bigotry against colour-blindness while prescribing no route map for how we get from one to the other'. While this is debatable, it highlights a point already considered, namely that hope is sometimes understood to be distinct from, even antithetical to, action. Why, then, suggest that to 'carry' a dream also includes the sense of 'carrying' understood as achieving or realising something?

Here is where 'infecting' can be understood as a critical component for realising a dream. In their study of music and social movements, Eyerman and Jameson describe how, strategic, instrumentally planned action on the one hand, and affect, aesthetic sensibility and emotion, on the other, are in fact not separate and should not be bifurcated in thinking about how change happens. This theory of action enriches our understanding of the emotional bases of cognition and problem solving, and the importance of, as discussed earlier, projection—culture creation—to change pathways.

Brian Keenan's point about the complementary of hope and planning touches on this theme. It is a theme well developed in music and arts therapies, and in studies of collective trauma and will be explored thoroughly in Chapter 4. For now, what is important is that the activity of hoping, understood as 'carrying' in all of the senses explored so far, involves imaginative engagement with, and creation of culture for, scenarios down the line. This is why I suggested, in Chapter 1, that hopefulness was a highly creative way of being. Through imaginative engagement, as we shall see, things do, really, and can, really, change. They change every time we engage with the images that hope projects because this activity, whether taking place singly or collectively, changes us; it recalibrates us emotionally, spiritually, cognitively in ways that leave us better poised for action and better equipped, mentally, spiritually, poised to take action, should the opportunity arise. In Chapter 4 this issue is explored in more detail and in ways that explore the incremental progress that the activity of hoping can achieve, even in very extreme situations.

This exploration will by no means be a paean to the power of positive thinking. Hope can be, as Nietzsche observed, uncomfortable. But while hope may not bring comfort, it may be necessary if we are attempting to realise a dream (including the dream that we do not abandon a dream); indeed, to hope is to engage in activity oriented to that realisation. Hope is necessary because, as we shall see, it can expand repertoires of thought and potential action by exercising our capacity for imaginative engagement. More immediately, hope is also necessary to our wellbeing while we endure things in the present. Insofar as hope remains committed to a dream, or alternate vision of how things could be and what they could become, hope is a refusal to capitulate. In this sense hope is never passive; to the contrary, hope is a strategy of refusal and rebellion, a way of resisting what otherwise 'is'. And insofar as hope—as has been argued— can keep us motivated and resourceful—in relation to what we might dream of, and thus ready to work when and how we can, hope has been identified as a health resource. In what ways, then, might hope be health-promoting and when in fact do we need to look more critically at what hope does for health?

References

Atkinson, P. (2020). *Writing Ethnographically*. London: Sage.

Back, L. (2015). Blind Pessimism and the Sociology of Hope. *Discovering Sociology*, Issue 27. Retrieved on April 12 from https://discoversociety.org/2015/12/01/blind-pessimism-and-the-sociology-of-hope/.

Bloch, E. (1986). *The Principle of Hope* (Vols. 1–3). Cambridge, MA: The MIT Press.

Bloch, E. (2000). *The Spirit of Utopia*. Palo Alto: Stanford University Press.

Brown, J. (2003). *Ernst Bloch and the Utopian Imagination*. Eras. Retrieved on May 30, 2020 from https://www.monash.edu/arts/philosophical-historical-international-studies/eras/past-editions/edition-five-2003-november/ernst-bloch-and-the-utopian-imagination#notes1.

Casey, E. (2000). *Remembering: A Phenomenological Study* (2nd ed.). Bloomington and Indianapolis, IN: Indiana University Press.

DeNora, T. (1995). *Beethoven and the Construction of Genius: Aesthetic Politics in Vienna 1790–1803.* Berkeley, Los Angeles and London: Unveristy of California Press.

DeNora, T. (2014). *Making Sense of Reality: Culture and Perception in Everyday Life.* London: Sage.

Eyerman, R. (2019). *Memory, Trauma and Identity.* Basingstoke: Palgrave Macmillan.

Eyerman, R., & Jameson, A. (1998). *Music and Social Movements.* Cambridge: Cambridge University Press.

Fine, G. A. (2012). *Tiny Publics: A Theory of Group Action and Culture.* New York: Russel Sage Foundation.

Gibbs, A. (2001). *Contagious Feelings: Pauline Hanson and the Epidemiology of Affect.* Australian Humanities Review Retrieved on June 24, 2020 from http://australianhumanitiesreview.org/2001/12/01/contagious-feelings-pauline-hanson-and-the-epidemiology-of-affect/.

Güran-Aydin, P., & DeNora, T. (2016). Remembering Through Music: Turkish Diasporic Identities in Berlin. In A. L. Tota & T. Hagen (Eds.), *Routledge International Handbook of Memory Studies* (pp. 233–246). London: Routledge.

Hagen, T. (2019). *Living in the Merry Ghetto: The Music and Politics of the Czech Underground.* Oxford: Oxford University Press.

Hatfield, E., Carpenter, M., & Rapson, R. L. (2014). Emotional Contagion as a Precursor to Collective Emotions. In C. Von Scheve & M. Salmela (Eds.), *Collective Emotions: Perspectives from Psychology, Philosophy and Sociology.* Oxford: Oxford University Press.

Hauge, O. H. (2019). *Det er den draumen.* Oslo: Det Norske Samlaget.

Hennion, A., & Méadel, C. (1989). The Artisans of Desire: The Mediation of Advertising Between Product and Consumer. *Sociological Theory, 7*(2), 191–209.

Herwig, C., & Brune, A. (2019). *Hope in Their Hands: Refugee Children Share Their Keepsakes.* Unicef. Retrieved on March 24, 2020 from https://www.unicef.org/stories/hope-their-hands-refugee-children-share-their-keepsakes.

Joas, H. (2000). *The Genesis of Values.* Chicago: University of Chicago Press.

Keenan, B. (1993). *An Evil Cradling.* London: Vintage.

Levitas, R. (2010 [1990]). *The Concept of Utopia.* Oxford: Peter Lang.

Mankowitz, Z. W. (2002). *Life Between Memory and Hope: The Survivors of the Holocaust in Occupied Germany.* Cambridge: Cambridge University Press.

McKesson, D. (2017). *On the Other Side of Freedom: The Case for Hope.* Penguin Books.

Miller, D. (2010). *Stuff*. Cambridge: Polity.

Mollison, J., & Gibson, M. (2015). See the Objects Refugees Carry on Their Journey to Europe. *Time Magazine*. Retrieved on March 24, 2020 from https://time.com/4062180/james-mollison-the-things-they-carried/.

Mühlhoff, R. (2019). Affective Resonance. In J. Slaby & C. von Scheve (Eds.), *Affective Societies: Key Concepts* (pp. 189–199). London: Routledge.

Nilsen, A. (1999). Where Is the Future? Time and Space as Categories in Analyses of Young People's Images of the Future. *Innovation: The European Journal of Social Science Research, 12*(2) 175–194.

Petersen, A. (2015). *Hope in Health: The Socio-Politics of Optimism*. Basingstoke: Palgrave Macmillan.

Prechtl, M. M. (1974). *Poster for G. Schirmer Music Company*. Retrieved on April 24, 2020 from https://www.lofty.com/products/vintage-1974-g-sch irmer-music-store-original-poster-featuring-beethoven-by-michael-prechtl-1-8xfhb.

Ruud, E. (2002). Music as a Cultural Immunogen: Three Narratives on the Use of Music as a Technology of Health. In I. M. Hanken, S. G. Nielsen, & M. Nerland (Eds.), *Research in and for Higher Music Education: Festschrift for Harald Jørgensen* (pp. 109–120). Oslo: Norwegian Academy of Music.

Ruud, E. (2008). Music in Therapy: Increasing Possibilities for Action. *Music and Arts in Action, 1*(1), 46–60.

Ruud, E. (2020). *Toward a Sociology of Music Therapy: Musicking as a Cultural Immunogen*. Dallas, TX: Barcelona Publishers.

Slaby, J., & von Scheve C. (Eds.). (2019). *Affective Societies: Key Concepts*. London: Routledge.

Stern, D. N. (2018 [1985]). *The Interpersonal World of the Infant*. London: Routledge.

Terpe, S. (2014). Negative Hopes: Social Dynamics of Isolating and Passive Forms of Hope. *Sociological Research Online*. Retrieved on March 25, 2020 from https://journals.sagepub.com/doi/full/10.5153/sro.3799?casa_token= ppAC6_V2nkAAAAA%3AIlDeGczr7_6ciZfSMkxpdPU1agACHQHf0L XN62fHgkO1UH0riejmkix_K6RajJfjd2XryyxUVyE.

Thompson, E. (2017). *Waking, Dreaming, Being: Self and Consciousness*. New York: Colombia University Press.

Tota, A. L. (2001). Homeless Memories: How Societies Forget Their Past. *Studies in Communication Sciences, 1*, 193–214.

Tota, A. L. (2004). Ethnographying Public Memory: The Commemorative Genre for the Victims of Terrorism in Italy. *Qualitative Research, 4*(2), 131–159.

Tota, A. L. (2005). Counter Memories of Terrorism: The Public Inscription of a Traumatic Past. In M. Jacobs & N. Hanrahan (Eds.), *The Blackwell Companion to the Sociology of Culture* (pp. 272–285). Oxford: Blackwells.

Waite, T. (1993). *Taken on Trust*. London: Hodder and Stoughton.

Witkin, R. W. (1974). *The Intelligence of Feeling*. Portsmouth, NH: Heinemann Educational Publishers.

Younge, G. (2013). *The Speech: The Story Behind Martin Luther King's Dream*. Chicago: Haymarket Books.

3

Hope, Health and Wellbeing

Taking a cue from Hagen's study of underground culture in the former Czechoslovakia, in this chapter I consider the interrelationship between hoping, health, and wellbeing. Hagen's work was itself inspired by that of Even Ruud whose pioneering work on music and wellbeing understands musical practice as a kind of 'cultural immunogen' (Ruud 2002, 2020). Ruud's work, which will be explored more fully in Chapter 4, serves here to introduce an important topic of research in recent years within bio-medical and neurological research but also in the humanities and health humanities (Crawford et al. 2015, 2020)—the mind–body–culture nexus.

In one of the starkest examples of this connection, the Austrian neurologist and psychologist, Viktor Frankl movingly described his experience of the constant terror of life in a concentration camp. In particular, Frankl's account speaks of hope and faith in the future as a way of promoting the body's resistance to disease. Frankl calls this practice 'psychohygeine' (Frankl 2004: 84). There are now several branches of interdisciplinary inquiry devoted to this theme that highlight the importance of psycho-cultural experience for physical and mental health. And from within that perspective, hope—understood as a psycho-cultural

T. DeNora, *Hope*,
https://doi.org/10.1007/978-3-030-69870-6_3

experience, can itself be seen as a condition of health. It is worth considering briefly four of the key perspectives on mind–body–culture here (psychoneuroimmunology, cultural immunogens, placebo effect, positive psychology), because they set the stage for considering, critically, the question of how, why, when, and to what extent, hope may support wellbeing and health.

3.1   Psychoneuroimmunology

The relatively recent field of psychoneuroimmunology—abbreviated as PNI—is focused on the interaction between mental processes and physical states. With antecedents in holistic models of mind–body that extend back over two millennia (Solomon 2002), PNI has been devoted to exploring, in empirically verifiable ways, the 'string of nerve, cell, muscle and chemical interactions, the implications of which are still being uncovered' (Fancourt 2014: 169). While PNI encompasses mental and physical health (indeed the point is that these are inseparable), programmatically research in PNI has centred on interactions between emotional triggers, neurological responses and the production of anti-bodies (bodily proteins that neutralize bacteria and viruses, otherwise known as pathogens). That interaction has been described as a cyclical feedback loop, a 'string of interactions between psychological processes, the brain and the immune system' (ibid). The idea is that the body's immune system is boosted when individuals are not distressed, and when they feel positive emotions such as happiness and contentment, which release endorphins into the blood. Equally importantly, when the immune system is in good working order, conversely, people are more likely to feel positive emotions. The process is circular.

While this model might sound mechanistic (one 'system' affecting the other) its actual workings are synergistic, in other words, there are looping mechanisms which are highly minute and constantly, mutually responding to, and constituting, each other. This is to say that seemingly 'different' systems are in fact mutually dependent; they co-produce each other and coalesce each instant within us to produce our immediate state of health and wellbeing and in ways that call into question the more modern bifurcation of mental and physical illness. By contrast physical and mental phenomena may be mutually causative, as in the case here described of chronic inflammation understood as:

> …a shared and common mechanism of both mental and physical illness. For example, psychiatric disorders like schizophrenia, bipolar disorder, major depression, and anxiety disorders have higher prevalence rates across a spectrum of autoimmune conditions compared to the general population. Additionally, subclinical immunological abnormalities are observed in a variety of psychiatric conditions, with chronic inflammation most extensively studied in the pathophysiology of depression. These observations blur the historical distinctions between mental and physical illness, yet clinical practice remains fragmented and primarily focused on differentially treating individual symptoms. (Alessi and Bennett 2020)

The implications of this research are that mental health conditions may, *in some circumstances,* arise in response to physiological conditions—inflammation for example—and vice versa.

As a brief aside, and before proceeding with this theme, it is important to note that I have taken care to say, 'in some circumstances', because mental health conditions may at times be attributed to individuals (and self-attributed) for a range of social reasons and which have identity politics. These politics point in turn to the importance of considering the social history of diagnosis—long-term but also in terms of individuals' diagnoses—as a matter for critical scrutiny. The point is that some, but not necessarily all, cases of mental health conditions may very well be interactively connected to biological conditions and the greater point is that feelings that manifest themselves in features or symptoms of mental health conditions may both arise and give rise to physical health conditions.

According to Alessi and Bennett, nonsteroidal anti-inflammatory drugs (NSAIDs), because they can diminish inflammation and reduce inflammatory markers, may offer effective treatment for depression and thus their work proposes an interdependency of mind (here mental states and conditions) and body (here inflammation due to heavy release of stressor hormones). While these conclusions may not be uncontroversial, and while, as a sociologist, I would suggest that they require further critical consideration (in particular around the question of 'what' mental illness is—its ontology, its aetiology and its social relations [DeNora 2017]), at the same time their findings prompt us to think carefully about mind–body interactions, in particular, interactions between stress, physiological responses and mental health.

So, the reasoning goes, if forms of action in the world lead to stress, then forms of action in the world can contribute to inflammation and therefore mental illness. Conversely, therefore, it is also to say that if forms of action in the world lead to the opposite of distress—relief, ease—then forms of action in the world can contribute to mental well-being. It is, specifically, the circularity of these processes that is of interest here. Thinking about this circularity in turn prompts thinking about non-pharmacological mechanisms for diminishing distress (and perhaps inflammation) and promoting wellbeing.

3.2   Cultural Immunogens

It is here that Ruud's (2002, 2020) notion of 'cultural immunogens' comes to the fore. For Ruud, cultural immunogens include health-promoting behaviours practices such as not smoking, avoiding addictive drugs (pharmaceutical or street drugs), drinking alcohol in moderation, avoiding overly-processed foods, eating fresh fruit, vegetables, drinking water, taking exercise. These practices are—one might suggest—mostly behavioural. But cultural immunogens also include meaningful practices and engagement with meaningful and aesthetic materials. Such engagement, Ruud suggests, can lead to lower levels of stress and distress, and higher levels of pleasure, confidence, fulfilment, sociability and social engagement. All of these 'immunogenic' practices can help to break the negative cycle of stress > activation of immune response > inflammation > weakened immune system > illness > stress. (Though it would be dangerous to assume that these *individual* practices are 'all it takes' to remain well and Ruud is quick to observe that there are matters extending beyond individuals which also fuel the circular loop of distress and illnesses. These things include poverty, pollution and toxic waste, dangerous work practices, violence and abuse, symbolic violence, and disempowerment.)

I will return to the interchange between health-promoting activities and wellbeing/illness in Chapter 4, considering the connections between cultural practice, health/wellbeing, and hopefulness. Meanwhile, and importantly, recognising stress as a determinant of illness, through the mechanisms just described (and probably many others not described), recognises illness as arising from mind–body–culture interactions. The point for now is that if the focus within PNI on mind–body–culture offers a scientific basis for a more holistic understanding of health and wellbeing, mental/physical, it also paves the way for a far more complex, interdisciplinary understanding of our biological and phys-iological conditions and the causative processes through which those conditions arise.

It is here that space opens in which to consider the importance of things outside of us—external to our minds/bodies and their 'input' to the looping processes just described. What we 'carry' in the five senses of carrying that I have described will affect our levels of 'immunity', cultur-ally (as explored in the previous chapter) and physiologically. But before we explore the hope-health interrelationship it is worth taking a step back to set health in context of a trans-disciplinary understanding of health-illness aetiology. This context offers ways of accounting for how illnesses and states of wellbeing/health emerge and take shape. It considers, in other words, their determinants or the mechanisms responsible for health and illness pain and its absence. A third perspective that can enrich this exploration is directed to the so-called Placebo-Effect.

3.3   The Placebo Effect

In the last ten years in the medical research literature, there has been a resurgence of interest in the so-called 'placebo' effect. A placebo is a substance or procedure that is deemed to be inert, to have no effect or 'active ingredient'—a sugar pill instead of a pain medication for example—that nonetheless works as if it were a 'real' medicine. (For example, in clinical trials the sugar pill performs well, perhaps as, or nearly as well as an actual analgesic would in giving relief from pain.) Within the PNI framework, of course, there is plenty of scope for the study of placebos and this includes a focus on the interaction between belief, faith and real-world effectiveness. Once the 'mind–body' dualism is set aside, the idea of the placebo can not only seem plausible but can seem worthy of concerted research. Indeed, one researcher has put it (notably quite a while ago), 'within a paradigm that is not based on the Cartesian dualism of body and mind there would not be any placebo effect to explain' (Ekeland, 1997: 77).

Interest in the placebo effect has, as with PNI, been linked to a much wider interdisciplinary concern with the interactions between mind, body, and culture. These concerns share a commitment to the ways that conditions, capacities and states associated with health/illness are not the property of individual beings but take shape relationally, and in ways that rely upon contextual affordances for being, feeling, sensing and acting separately and together. They highlight how even at the deepest level of physiology and sensation things take shape in spatial, temporal and situational contexts that include also the ways in which those things come to be named and addressed as 'problems', 'solutions', 'treatments' and 'interventions'.

And interest in placebo effects extends into the popular domain. An article in *Psychology Today* (March 2018) entitled, 'Placebo Effect: Evidence suggests that placebo effects are becoming more powerful' describes how antidepressants often fail to outperform placebos in Randomised Clinical Trials. From around 2010 newspapers and popular scientific media began to detail the various, often surprising results of placebo research, even including so-called 'sham' surgery procedures:

> …53 randomized controlled trials that included placebo surgery as one option. In more than half of them, though, the effect of sham surgery was equivalent to that of the actual procedure. The authors noted, though, that with the exception to the studies on osteoarthritis of the knee and internal mammary artery ligation noted above, 'most of the trials did not result in a major change in practice. (Caroll 2014)

This popular article can be seen to disseminate what is now a growing area of research in medicine, for example this trail reported in the *British Medical Journal* in 2014:

> The majority of the trials showed an improvement in the surgical group as well as in the placebo group, which would suggest that some surgical procedures may have a placebo effect and that some of the benefits of surgery are related to factors other than the crucial surgical element. (Wartolowska et al. 2014)

In simple language, the placebo process seems to work because of the ways that expectations trigger what are called 'reward pathways' in the brain which in turn trigger various, disease-specific 'downstream' physiological effects. These 'downstream' effects may include the release of the body's own opioid compounds, dopamine, and serotonin (the 'feel good' chemicals that are released in fact when we do 'feel good', i.e., experience beauty and pleasure and the absence of stress) and/or also physiological changes such as cardio-vascular (our heartrate slows), respiratory (we breath more deeply), nervous (we are calmer), and gastro-intestinal (digestive processes function more easily) (Polich et al. 2018).

* * *

The twentieth century New Jersey poet and physician, William Carlos Williams described how, on his house calls he tried, 'to leave the visited figuring that maybe a door has been opened, and the visitor (me, the doc doing his job) feeling he's gotten the picture right, and so was of good use. Some service done' (Coles and Roma 2008: 86). Thinking that the 'doc' has 'gotten the picture right' provides in turn a ground for hope and thus a 'service'. In a consideration of hope in relation to health, physician Jerome Groopman recounts examples from his long career of how, as he puts it, 'realistic' hopes can help physiological processes of healing. And in ways that are akin to the placebo effect. Hope, Groopman suggests, lies at, 'the very heart of healing' (2006: 212).

Groopman describes how a placebo process involves real effects physiologically (Groopman 2006: 173). And the placebo is much more than, 'mind over matter'. Rather, it highlights mind and matter so closely coupled that it may be impossible to distinguish between the two. If we expect to gain relief from a procedure, a ritual and/or a substance, our bodies, it seems, cooperate and documentable neurochemical processes are set in motion. From a sociological perspective, of interest is how these mind/body interactions happen and in what ways are cultural practices involved?

It seems that the term 'expectation' here is key, as is the three-fold timeframe to which expectation contributes. While expectation is a state of mind involving more certainty than hope, it is also future-oriented. Equally important is that the sense of certainty that the placebo seeks to encourage itself contributes to an altered health-state. The sense that something good will happen as a result of taking a pill, or submitting to surgery can, in other words, actually trigger the body's endogenous responses and in ways that 'really work' to suppress pain, reduce mental distress, or in relation to mental health—just help.

What has not yet been explored is how the specific practices associated with hoping as an activity may be contribute to placebo effects. How for example do people—together and/or separately—enhance expectation through what they 'carry' into situations of healthcare and healing, and how does the social dynamics of interaction with others contribute to that process ('this will pass in time' someone might say to you, or 'give this treatment time and you will improve'). How, moreover, do people 'protect' their hope during processes of treatment or recuperation, and how are hopes 'projected' into contexts of care, to what extent can this be seen to be a collaborative process, one that comes to be linked to processes of mutual infection, when hopes are diffused among a group? In what ways, in other words, might carrying the dream of getting better, of managing pain, actually contribute to that dream's realisation? These questions as just posed are empirical questions that can, and arguably should, be studied as part of a research program of hope practices understood as cultural immunogens—and that means an explicit focus on the cultures of hope. I shall develop this focus in detail in Chapters 4 and 5.

The focus on expectation, faith, and hope as cultural immunogens is a focus on how and where habits of mind and cognitive patterns come from and how they are sustained. It is also a focus on how we develop and maintain our sense of certainty and in a stable and secure reality where we may, reasonably, expect certain things to happen and where it is reasonable also to hope for things to happen, or that things 'just might' happen. In this sense, expectation, at the heart of the placebo process, can be understood from within the terms of a fourth perspective, positive psychology and its focus on coherence.

3.4 Positive Psychology—Positive, and Negative

The key proponent of positive psychology, medical sociologist, Aaron Antonovsky, describes what he views as 'salutogenic' factors, that is things that can promote health and wellbeing (Antonovsky 1987). According to Antonovsky, a critical feature of wellbeing is an individual's sense of coherence, and, more generally, meaning in life. Adjacent to coherence and meaning, and indeed a prerequisite for them, is, in Antonovsky's term, 'ontological security' or the sense of oneself as secure in the world and in a predictable, reliable world within which it is possible to act, to establish coherent patterns of activity over time. How individuals, and groups, can acquire a sense of ontological security, coherence and meaning is of course a question for cultural sociology. The interrelation between culture—in particular the arts—and health is a currently growing area in health studies and health humanities (Daykin 2020; Crawford et al. 2020). It is also central, as we have explored earlier, to what Ruud terms 'cultural immunogens' (Ruud 2002, 2020). I return to this theme in Chapter 4.

To be sure, hoping can enhance a person's sense of coherence. Hoping should, in other words, be counted as a cultural immunogen. It can be understood to contribute to the complex strand of body–mind chain reactions that produce wellness and/or illness. For this reason, hope has been a topic within the psychology and sociology of health and illness. How the hope-wellbeing nexus is considered, however, is itself a topic for critical sociology.

The psychologist Gary Snyder has suggested that a hopeful personality is associated both with success and with disease prevention. Rejecting the conception of hope as an emotion, Snyder views hope as a motivational state and thus as preparation for action. Snyder is perhaps most well-known for his three-part understanding of hope as goals, pathways to meet those goals, and agency or belief that goals can be reached. It is the belief that one can reach one's goals, then, that Snyder recognises as hope. Within this version of hope theory, hope is understood as a quantifiable, measurable entity and a property of individuals. Snyder's work has therefore included contributions to the development of different versions of hope assessment instruments (The Trait Hope Scale, State Hope Scale, Children's Hope Scale). These instruments are designed to gauge how able individuals consider themselves to be at generating routes or pathways to goals (pathway questions) and how strongly an individual believes him or herself to be motivated to achieve goals (the 'I can do this' feeling), understood in turn as, 'agency thinking'.

Snyder and his colleagues suggest that people who score high on one of the Hope Scale are also more likely to have better health, for two reasons. First, they are more likely, regardless of educational attainment, to engage with and use information about disease prevention and second, they are more likely to comply with medical advice, if they fall ill:

> Hope has been related to better adjustment in conditions involving chronic illness, severe injury, and handicaps…Once ill, people with high versus low hope appear to remain appropriately energised and focused on what they need to do in order to recuperate. This is in stark contrast to the counter-productive self-focus and self-pity…that can overtake people with low hope. This self-pity increases anxiety and compromises the healing process…(Snyder et al. 2018: 34)

The hope-health nexus articulated in terms of individuals' dispositions to hope highlights hope's role as a motivating factor for health promotion and healthy behaviours. People with high levels of hope, it is suggested, are more likely to take action to reduce future health problems—physical activity, smoking cessation, or dietary change are typical examples offered. But, and despite its focus on activism, and despite the obvious good intentions of this perspective, looking at hope individualistically risks lending support to discourses that 'blame the victim' for health misfortunes (e.g., it is the individual's problem if they do not engage in pro-health behaviours). This risk is connected to how individualistic conceptions of hope and health often sidestep how individuals' life circumstances may contribute to particular 'lifestyle' 'choices', and I have already considered this question in Chapter 1 in relation to Berlant's discussion of 'slow death'. Additionally, as I will discuss below, individualistic conceptions of hope and health fail to consider how the forms that hopes assumes (what they hope for and how they hope) is mediated by economic and political interests and concerns. (For example, I might find it difficult to hope for health because of the need to engage routinely in high risk activities related to my job. Or, conversely, you, by virtue of your social resources, status, age, ethnicity, or gender, may be better equipped to hope than I.) As such, individualistic—personality-centred—perspectives on hope overlook the social, material and psychological activities and situations in which hope is kindled and sustained (and the wider contextual issues that may lead individuals to feel distress and despair, as discussed earlier).

Nonetheless, the idea that a hopeful outlook may be useful as part of a strategy of pain management and recovery is intriguing and should not be ignored. That idea also returns us to the issues broached in the discussion above of PNI and the placebo effect. And it points to the forms of activity that can be explored in relation to, and which produce the effects associated with, alleviating pain.

The theory for why hope can support pain tolerance is that hope shifts attention from pain to goals (Rasmussen et al. 2018: 162). In other words, we train our mental focus on (or 'project' into our consciousness and perhaps also into shared social space) visions of where we dream about being in the future, down the line. This dream, and its future-orientation, becomes a focal point: it masks, or displaces from consciousness, more present-oriented awareness of on-going pain. So-called, high hope individuals, according to Rasmussen, approached pain and the source of pain with different expectations from those who had less hope. Additionally, the latter group were more likely to engage in what is called, 'pain catastrophising', that is they engaged in an exaggerated negative response both to pain and the expectation of pain (ibid).

As with the placebo effect, if you expect something to hurt (catastrophizing), *it probably will hurt* (and hurt a lot more than when attention is otherwise engaged). This kind of negative feedback loop is often termed a 'nocebo' (the opposite of placebo); it can be explored in terms of the cognitive and embodied practices through which it is produced: at the thought of 'this hurts' or 'this is going to hurt' one tenses, and, equally importantly, directs one's attention to the sensations one 'expects' to feel. This focus in turn elevates stress hormones and reduces resilience to endure. The mind is not distracted but, to the contrary, hyper-focused on negative sensations and thoughts. Whereas when engaged in hoping (that things will improve, that time will heal) the mind is not distracted but redirected, and with potentially 'real' consequences for pain because the pain is now lodged within a narrative where, over time, it will abate. Just how far, then, can hope go toward ameliorating illness, and illness experience? And where might hope be of contended benefit? And finally, who may hope, which is to ask, in Groopman's words, why it is that some people find it easier to hold on to hope than others (Groopman 2006: 209)?

3.5   Hope as Resource, Hope as Liability

The research on connections between hope and cancer have thrown up findings that are both tantalising and contentious. These findings have ramifications for how we think about the role of hope in relation to life-threatening, and end of life, diseases more generally. Hope has not only been shown to be a factor in coping with cancer diagnosis, treatment and aftercare (for example in helping to lower distress and linked with fewer follow-up appointments linked to cancer-linked illnesses or issues) but also to lower fear that the disease will recur.

However, not all people living with cancer are, want, or are able, to be 'hopeful' about the future (Daykin et al. 2007: 365, 366). And some critics have pointed to the new 'regime' of hope within cancer cultures and illness cultures more widely. Within this perspective, hope is seen to be structured in ways that capture those individuals and place them on trajectories that support the interests and agendas of organisations and for-profit groups. They facilitate, as it is sometimes termed, 'patient compliance':

> For some, hope has been seen to provide a promotional basis for advancing nascent biomedical economies and enrolling potential investment both in terms of financialisation and also corporeally in terms of access to bodies and the support of patient advocacy groups (Brown 2003; Del Vecchio Good et al. 1990; Novas 2006). It has become important to recognise the extent to which hope has become a vector for the embodiment of, and indeed the embodied reproductivity of, promissory futures in fields as wide ranging as stem cell therapies (Petersen and Seear 2011), critical illness (Mattingly 2010) and fertility treatment (Franklin 1997)... (Brown 2015: 120)

Brown's use of the term 'advancing' and 'enrolling' highlight how, if I pin my hopes to a form the promise offered by a form of therapy, I may also be helping to support a biomedical-economic agenda that may, or may not, be in my interests. Thus, while there is considerable wisdom in the idea that hope and recovery are interrelated, there are also problems with simple equations of hope, understood as a trait or a state, and health. First, as have already described, there can be a strongly individualist tenor to 'hope theory' in relation to health. We have already seen hopefulness conceptualised as a 'personality trait' and an attribute of 'healthy' individuals. Second, the idea that, if you are a 'hopeful' person you are more likely to recover from illness because you are more likely to 'want' to receive the things (treatments, procedures, drugs) that medical science is able to offer, and you are more likely to accept medical advice and to endure medical procedures, overlooks how not all people, and not all illnesses fit this model of patient compliance.

For example, in a study of people recovering from a major stroke, researchers found that far from helping or motivating, hope was a source of distress:

> in almost every instance, the experience of stroke recovery over the longer term had not only left survivors with diminished horizons of self-expectation, but further, with an attitude in which the future was cast

as ominously threatening, and indeed as a matter best avoided both in thought and conversation (Alaszewski and Wilkinson 2014: 183)

To enjoin someone in such a position with glib phrases ('you must not give up hope') can be not only unrealistic but also uncaring in the sense that it allocates the burden of responsibility for getting better to the person who is ill. And it sidesteps how there may be adaptations that might open up new ways of living in novel and meaningful ways that do not necessarily include 'getting better'. These adaptations might be material—you decide it is finally time to use a wheelchair. But they may also be social: for example, the very friends and family who are urging you not to give up hope might themselves need to adapt their ways of speaking, their expectations of what can or should be done and together (which materially might include sharing out forms of assistance, reorganizing how collective activities happen, or even something as basic as how fast to move together and how to avoid needing to take the stairs).

Social adaptations also include what we might believe, reasonably, we 'can' hope for. As Scott (2009: 131), considering the study of health narratives, observes, 'we search for continuity and meaning and where there is none, we create it through retrospective narratives'. The creativity of realistic hoping involves, always, a two-way tinkering with what might and what can be attained as those narratives are adapted to specific constraints—in Oliver Sacks' (1991) sense, we 'accommodate' to the 'reality' of our circumstances. In the face of seemingly incurable illness, for example, we may revaluate what we hope for, for example, moving from the hope of recovery to the hope of reconciliation with family, or to the hope of diminished pain (Aldridge 2004: 102).

* * *

This realism is one that knows that under some circumstances it may be good to accept the possibility that things cannot change. These are not occasions for abandoning hope, but rather *adjusting* hope in light of changing circumstances, and adjusting psychologically, psychically and socially to new situations so as to take appropriate action (including the action that is inaction). And this adjustment is directly connected to our ability, individually and collectively, to innovate, culturally speaking, to

develop cultural forms that fit in more bespoke ways, the complex realities of health/illness conditions and that help us to gain leverage on
otherwise often intransigent views and unyielding conditions, conven-
tions and regulations about how we live, and are 'supposed' to live, with
health/illness issues.

Medical sociologists have observed that sometimes people who suffer
chronic back pain from unknown causes can actually find consolation
and psychological relief when they finally learn the cause of their pain,
even when the prognosis is poor (Hilbert 1986). The comfort comes
from, finally, being able to understand your pain in terms of shared
meanings and categories, even when those diagnostic categories may spell
permanent disability, or even death. At that point—in the Zen sense
quoted earlier—the sense of being 'tired out' and able to rest arrives. And
you are literally then able to 'come to terms' with your pain—it is now
a known. At these times, urging someone to hope for remission (when
realistically it is unlikely) may not only be uncaring, it may be isolating.
And it may be selfish. It may be selfish because it absolves the speaker
from having to engage more fully with the other person's plight, skirting
the grimmer realities that not 'getting better' may involve, and curtailing
deeper (honest) communication. Extolling unrealistic virtues of hope is
not useful, and may cause harm, to people who are suffering. We take
care in what we hope for and what we uphold as what we (and who is
the 'we'?) 'should' be hoping for.

Hope, in other words, particularly when conceptualized as both the
property of individuals and also as their social responsibility (to give up
hope, to give up the 'fight' against cancer, for example, is to let others
down) is a means for enrolling individuals on to agendas that may, or
may not be, in their interests. In this respect, the psychology of hope
metrics has been accused of deleting nuance and breadth to thinking
about illness by reducing the equation between individual affect and
response to illness to a question about motivation, personality, and—
compliance; to return to Ehrenreich (discussed in Chapter 1), part of
the cult of positivity. For this reason, the psychology of hope and health
is viewed by some as part of the 'psy-complex' of governmentality, or,
'the attempt to regulate how people behave and think' (Parker 1997: 123
quoted in Brown 2015: 133).

This critical perspective is important. It also calls us to reflect on our own everyday impulses and speech acts since we may speak the discourse of hope often unthinkingly, or rather, it may speak us. It is here where hope can quickly descend into glib optimism and in ways that can override the more tragic features of experience and reasons for hoping:

> Psychologist, C.R. Snyder and his colleagues say that hope is cultivated when we have a goal in mind, determination that a goal can be reached, and a plan on how to reach those goals. In this sense, we can hope for big things (e.g., the Presidency) or we can hope for small things (e.g., a clean room). Although people who have hope will have a sense of determination and a plan on how to achieve these goals, they will also be flexible, understanding that they may need to have a couple backup plans in case the first one doesn't work out. Like the little engine that could, they keep telling themselves "I think I can, I think I can" (Goldstein 2008: n.p.)

3.6   Hope Understood as 'Tragic'

The 'little engine that could' is a story about optimism, not hope. And while we should not reject the hope-health interrelationship, it is important also to retain the sense of hope as 'tragic', or at least, as laden with ambivalence. Following Ehrenreich in the attempt to develop a 'realistic' understanding of hope as an activity, we need to appreciate hope as part of a clouded, ambiguous and sometimes contradictory picture of feelings impulses and values, a picture that is painted with too broad a brush, and with too bright a palette, by hope's statisticians and by the imagery of the 'little engine'. Over-simplification of hope as 'being positive', coupled with a preoccupation to measure people's individual dispositions to hope, and thereby their emotional lives, can, I suggest, be harmful. To suggest that each of us possesses a measurable 'hope score' potentially degrades complex lived experience. It also, potentially, does symbolic violence to that experience if it implies that it can offer an accurate picture of who we are (since the complexity of our lives spills out beyond the containers that statistical parameters can capture). And if we identify with, and internalize, those pictures of ourselves that statistical scales provide ('I am a moderately hopeful person'), we may end up colluding with, and compounding, that symbolic violence.

Thus, the focus on 'hope regimes' and 'hope scales' highlights how hoping is a topic for critical sociology. It suggests that undue focus on hope as a personality trait or characteristic can leave hope, as a process, black-boxed, overlooked. For example, we know nothing at all about what it might mean to 'become' hopeful in relation to health and illness, or how, in those contexts, how people come to embark upon hopeful trajectories of action and thought (or how they do not). We learn nothing of a person-specific nature about how and why people hope, about the resources that it might take to kindle hope, or about how people embark upon projects of carrying hope (a dream) in time and place. And yet, these questions may have direct bearing upon people's health and they may also be linked to the ways that people's situation in relation to culture may help or hamper their 'ability' to hope, to 'bear' a dream. Adjacent to this concern, as we have already considered, is the question of *whose* dreams or projects are being carried and how this may be subject to negotiation adjustment and change over the course of the journey.

Thus hope, understood as an activity, is a fundamentally social project even while it is personal. It is an activity that locates and appropriates resources for the carrying of the dream in question. Those resources include what we bring and protect and project, and what infects us, for example, which vocabularies that circulate in the public domain, or within smaller circles, do we employ when we speak about what we hope for? And how might they shift over time and in relation to circumstance?

A personal example: when my father, shortly after my mother's death, was diagnosed with lung cancer at age 87 (the tumour was already very large), his first response was, 'I'm going to fight this', and his first impulse was to ask about whether he could immediately be scheduled for surgery (he could not). In the end, he did not so much 'fight' the disease as find a way to live with it. And what he, indeed we, came to hope for was also different—we hoped for meaningful time together until the end. We hoped that death would not be painful or protracted when it came. These were hopes we were able to realise, thanks to the support of many people, and organisations (including my employer who allowed me to take a leave of absence, including the Hospice team in my father's community, including the friends and neighbours who visited daily, including many other things…).

What happened was different: my father did not 'beat' cancer; he died one year after first being diagnosed. But during that year he and we experienced many heightened communicative situations, many richly creative acts under the guise of card playing, television watching, music listening (DeNora 2012). After an aluminum ramp was installed and the weather warmed up, we went outside and sat together in the front (street-facing) garden (the back garden was inaccessible). This in turn drew visits from neighbours would walk over for a cup of coffee (or glass of wine) and a chat. As these gatherings took place in suburban New Jersey, and, because social events out in the front of a house were unconventional, they drew notice and drew more people in (and not out of a sense of 'duty' but for sheer pleasure—it became 'fun' to be out front, waving to passing cars, sitting in folding metal chairs). My father enjoyed this socializing immensely, coming out of the house, often, in pajama bottoms and a NY Yankees tee shirt, and sitting in front of his house next to the shrubs he had planted nearly fifty years before. When he died the following winter, the funeral directors were willing to wait while many of his friends and family members came to the house to pay their last respects. One might say that, all things considered, we got what, realistically, we had hoped for and for that reason, and despite the inevitable grief, this death also involved a kind of joy—in what had been achieved (collectively, in terms of social bonding and meaning) during that last year of my father's life.

* * *

One might only in extreme circumstances ever hope for death, but one might hope for a connected and 'whole' last phase of life and in this way hope's future is a foreshortened interval of time. It is important, in other words, to consider what hope hopes for, and what is a worthy object of hope if hope is not to be reduced to blind optimism. In this, it helps if realism is projected into the shared atmosphere, if, for example, physicians are candid (which can be difficult for them emotionally speaking). When we visited my father's physician for news after his initial biopsy (in company with his closest friend, then 89 and previously treated for cancer himself) the doctor sat us down and said, 'you know what? You're pretty old now and if this thing doesn't get you, something else might'. While that might sound, out of context, harsh or flippant, it was not, and it was taken with equanimity; the two old men looked with great respect at the 'young' doctor (who was, at a guess, in his early forties) and agreed that he was making a very good point. Two or three generations ago, when death was less of a stranger to culture (in days past corpses would have been kept at home for viewing and the night after a death involved a period of 'watching' [Jewett 1890]) a statement such as the one this doctor made would not have been strange. Instead, it would have been treated with respect, deemed, and without undue emotion, as the inevitable if solemn recognition that a point had been reached in the span of a long life. Quoting the poet Roethke ('in a dark time the eye begins to see' [Taylor 2018: 72]) Ros Taylor has described how, for many people—but not all—'accepting a negative reality, can open new vistas' (ibid):

> Acceptance of death is a possibility unleashes possibilities for better endings and a different set of hopes: hopes about how to spend time, hopes for the future of the family, hope for a pain-free death, hope to be yourself. But it can also unleash feelings of pointlessness and a wish for a hastened death. (Taylor 2018: 72–73)

In context of 'end of life', hopes for the future may not involve changes in future circumstances—indeed they may be linked as Taylor observes, to hastened death. And they may be less concerned with the future and more concerned with reparation of the past. It is therefore a key question—*what kind of vista*, hope, as an activity, seeks to 'open up'? For example, we may hope we will be able to come to terms with some matter in our past, or reconcile a relationship, or forgive, or receive forgiveness. These things open up the possibility of 'control' over life before death as part of preparation for death. They open spaces for thinking about death, our death, and planning for events associated with it such as how and where to die, and what kind of funeral. Planning one's funeral need not be morose; indeed, it can be both creative, joyful (if not at the surface level, 'happy'). It can afford a sense of control, or, in Snyder's terms, 'agency'.

For all of these reasons linked to the complexity of people, people's lives and lived experiences, the politics of hoping, the idea that we can reduce hope to a quantitative property of individuals and then harness it to a plan for rehabilitation is an idea that conceptualizes hope too narrowly. It is also a conception that modulates too smoothly into bio-political rhetoric of the 'war on cancer' (which is not to say that discovering ways of preventing and curing cancer are not valued!) in in ways that pressure the cancer victim to comply with expectations that she or he will (need to) be 'hopeful'. From there, it is dangerously easy to slip into a way of thinking that implicitly blames the victim if treatment fails—he or she 'gave up', 'did not try hard enough', etc. Erased from this picture are all visions of how the medical procedures and science may themselves require further nuance, how treatments may affect people variously and how in fact treatments (medical but also so-called 'alternative') may be urged, and applied, in inappropriate ways when and if a profit motive is at stake. For these reasons, Peterson has observed that it is important to set the study of hope in context of its 'socio-politics' by which he means:

> ...the ways in which efforts to engender hope, including the particular objects (that which are 'hoped for') are bound up with broader projects oriented to shaping selves and society in particular ways (2015: 4).

* * *

Would it seem that we need to take a side? *Either* hopeful individuals have a greater tendency to be healthy and/or health promoting *or* that pressing individuals to behave in ways that are hopeful but also subservient to particular trajectories of treatment is a form of control? I would like to suggest that neither of these options is quite right. As Peterson (quoted above) puts it, we need to encourage hope while remaining critical of its origins. So, while it is true that discourses of hope have been exploited—intentionally and unintentionally—by various interested actors, at the same time there are good reasons why being hopeful can boost an individual's sense of coherence and therefore potentially dispel the condition that lead to mental/physical illness.

If hope can function as a kind of cultural immunogen (Ruud2002, 2020), then we need to attend to the question of where hope originates, the resources from which it is produced, how it takes its specific shapes in particular contexts, and how specific cultures of hope contribute to these processes. The next chapter begins to consider the role of cultural materials and resources for hoping. If hope is the activity of carrying a dream, where do dreams originate and how is hope, often understood as an anchoring activity, itself anchored? What, in other words, does culture do for hope?

References

Alaszewski, A., & Wilkinson, I. (2014). The Paradox of Hope for Working Age Adults Recovering from Stroke. *Health, 19*(2), 172–187.

Aldridge, D. (2004). *Health, the Individual and Integrated Medicine: Revisiting an Aesthetic of Health Care*. London: Jessica Kingsley Publishers.

Alessi, M. G., & Bennett, J. M. (2020). Mental Health Is the Health of the Whole Body: How Psychoneuroimmunology Can Inform & Improve Treatment. *Journal of Evaluation in Clinical Practice, 26*(5), 1539–1547.

Antonovsky, A. (1987). *Unraveling the Mystery of Health: How People Manage Stress and Stay Well*. San Francisco, CA: Jossey-Bass Publishers.

Brown, J. (2003). *Ernst Bloch and the Utopian Imagination*. Eras. Retrieved on May 30, 2020 from https://www.monash.edu/arts/philosophical-historical-international-studies/eras/past-editions/edition-five-2003-november/ernst-bloch-and-the-utopian-imagination#notes1.

Brown, N. (2015). Metrics of Hope: Disciplining Affect in Oncology. *Health, 2*(19), 119–136.

Caroll, A. E. (2014, October 6). The Placebo Effect Doesn't Apply Just to Pills. *New York Times*. Retrieved on March 29, 2020 from https://www.nytimes.com/2014/10/07/upshot/the-placebo-effect-doesnt-apply-just-to-pills.html.

Coles, R., & Roma, T. (2008). *House Calls with William Carlos Williams, MD*. New York: Power House Books.

Crawford, P. P., Brown, B., Baker, C., Tischler, V., & Abrams, B. (2015). *Health Humanities*. Basingstoke: Palgrave Macmillan.

Crawford, P., Brown, B., & Charise, A. (2020). *The Routledge Companion to Health Humanities*. London: Routledge.

Daykin, N. (2020). *Arts, Health and Wellbeing: A Critical Perspective on Research, Policy and Practice*. London: Routledge.

Daykin, N., McClean, S., & Bunt, L. (2007). Creativity, Identity and Healing: Participants' Accounts of Music Therapy in Cancer Care. *Health, 1*(3), 349–370.

DeNora, T. (2012). Resounding the Great Divide: Theorising Music in Everyday Life at the End of Life. *Mortality, 17*(2), 92–105.

DeNora, T. (2017). My Bonnie Dearie. In T. Stickley & S. Clift (Eds.), *Arts, Health, and Wellbeing: A Theoretical Inquiry for Practice* (pp. 85–106). Cambridge: Cambridge Scholars Press.

Ekeland, T.-J. (1997). The Healing Context and Efficacy in Psychotherapy: Psychotherapy and the Placebo Phenomenon. *International Journal of Psychotherapy, 2*(1), 77–87.

Fancourt, D. (2014). An Introduction to the Psychoneuroimmunology of Music: History, Future Collaboration and a Research Agenda. *Psychology of Music, 44*(2), 168–182.

Frankl, V. E. (2004 [1946]). *Man's Search for Meaning*. London: Ebury.

Goldstein, E. (2008). *Breaking down Barack Obama's Psychology of Hope and How It May Help You in Trying Times… A Blog About Mindfulness, Stress-Reduction, Psychotherapy and Mental Health*. Retrieved on April 6, 2020 from https://web.archive.org/web/20121110102512/http://www.mentalhelp.net/poc/view_doc.php?type=doc&id=28966&cn=110.

Good, M.-J. D., Good, B., Schaefer, C., & Lind, S. E. (1990). American Oncology and the Discourse on Hope. *Culture, Medicine and Psychiatry, 14*(1), 59–79.

Groopman, J. (2006). *The Anatomy of Hope: How People Prevail in the Face of Illness*. New York: Random House.

Hilbert, R. (1986). Anomie and the Moral Regulation of Reality: The Durkheimian Tradition on Modern Relief. *Sociological Theory, 4*(1), 1–19.

Jewett, S. O. (1890). Miss Tempy's Watchers. In *Tales of New England*. Boston: Houghton, Mifflin and Co.

Novas, C. (2006). The Political Economy of Hope: Patients' Organizations, Science and Biovalue. *BioSocieties, 1*(3), 289–305.

Parker, I. (1997). *Psychoanalytic Culture*. London: Sage.

Peterson, A. (2015). *Hope in Health: The Socio-Politics of Optimism*. Basingstoke: Palgrave Macmillan.

Polich, G., Iaccarino, M. A., Kaptchuk, T. J., Morales-Quezada, L., & Zafonte, R. (2018). Placebo Effects in Traumatic Brain Injury, *Journal of Neurotrauma, 1*, 35, 1205–1212. Retrieved on March 29, 2020 from https://www.ncbi.nlm.nih.gov/pubmed/29343158.

Rasmussen, H. N., O'Byrne, K. K., Vandment, M., & Pl Cole, B. (2018). *Hope and Physical Health*. In M. W. Gallagher & S. J. Lopez (Eds.), *The Oxford Handbook of Hope* (p. 159). Oxford: Oxford University Press.

Ruud, E. (2002). Music as a Cultural Immunogen: Three Narratives on the Use of Music as a Technology of Health. In I. M. Hanken, S. G. Nielsen, & M. Nerland (Eds.), *Research in and for Higher Music Education: Festschrift for Harald Jørgensen* (pp. 109–120). Oslo: Norwegian Academy of Music.

Ruud, E. (2020). *Toward a Sociology of Music Therapy: Musicking as a Cultural Immunogen*. Dallas, TX: Barcelona Publishers.

Sacks, O. (1991). *Awakenings*. London: Picador.

Scott, S. (2009). *Making Sense of Everyday Life*. Cambridge: Polity.

Solomon, G. F. (2002). The Development and History of Psychoneuroimmunology. In H. G. Koenig & H. J. Cohen (Eds.), *The Link Between Religion and Health: Psychoneuroimmunology and the Faith Factor* (pp. 31–42). Oxford, UK: Oxford University Press.

Snyder, G., Rand, K. L., & Sigmon, D. R. (2018). Hope Theory: A Member of the Positive Psychology Family. In M. W. Gallagher & S. J. Lopez (Eds.), *The Oxford Handbook of Hope* (pp. 27–45). Oxford: Oxford University Press.

Taylor, R. (2018). Relationship, Not Intervention: A Palliative Physician's Perspective. In A. Goodhead & N. Hartley (Eds.), *Spirituality in Hospice Care: How Staff and Volunteers Can Support the Dying and Their Famiies* (pp. 57–83). London: Jessica Kingsley Publications.

Wartolowska, K., Judge, A., Hopewell, S., Collins, G. S., Dean, B. J., Rombach, I., et al. (2014). Use of Placebo Controls in the Evaluation of Surgery: Systematic Review. *British Medical Journal, 348*. https://doi.org/10.1136/bmj.g3253.

4

Cultivating Dreams

Dreams can empower, and hope can lead to a sense of empowerment—for individuals and for groups. That empowerment in turn can keep us strong—and able to carry on carrying dreams. In Chapter 1, I described how hope involves five forms of 'carrying' a dream. But where do the dreams we dream come from, how do they take shape, grow and change, and how are they cultivated and sustained? For there will be times when we feel tired, desolate, rudderless, anchorless (the word *anchor* will have a new, sociological, salience in this chapter). At those times, our dream(s) may recede. The first question explored in this chapter therefore is what does it take, and what can we do, to keep a dream alive and in the forefront of our consciousness?

In a book devoted to Martin Luther King Junior's famous 'I have a dream' speech, Gary Younge describes how:

> King would call [Mahalia Jackson] when he felt down for some 'gospel music therapy' …'he would ask her to sing 'The Old Rugged Cross" or, "Jesus Met the woman at the Well" down the phone' (Younge 2013: 95–96)

© The Author(s), under exclusive license to Springer Nature Switzerland AG 2021
T. DeNora, *Hope*,
https://doi.org/10.1007/978-3-030-69870-6_4

Doctor King's need for 'music therapy', 'down the phone' highlights how carrying a dream, though it can empower, also has its own rhythm of changes, its ups and downs. So, what does it take to recharge when we are flagging or when the vision seems remote?

In King's case, that recharging required a connection to something cultural. Which in turn involved 'time out' from on-going work, a phone call, a request, and some time spent listening, re-charging. In this case, the cultural material was music (and as we will see music is often deeply implicated in helping people to stay connected to hopes and dreams). Key here is that the activity of holding on to hope, sustaining a dream, as McKesson (2017, quoted in Chapter 1) described, takes *work*. Part of that work involves turning to resources, such as music, to figure out what it is we are hoping for (we saw an example of this process in Chapter 2, as described by Eyerman and Jameson (1998) about the role Bob Dylan's music played in helping the leaders of SDS to identify the direction they were going in, 'next'). Another part of that work involves actively locating the things that will generate a sense of empowerment that simultaneously stokes hope and is produced through hoping. What, then, does it take to hope?

4.1   Musical Hope

In *How Music Helps*, music therapist Gary Ansdell writes about Nuri, suffering from chronic depression after experiencing political violence. Nuri tells Ansdell that he gets from music, 'some sort of hope…something fresh is coming. I have to carry on…'. Ansdell describes how, as he puts it:

> I've noticed over the years as a music therapist that hope is perhaps the most common if mysterious affordance of musicking – whether in everyday or more extreme situations. (2014: 275–276)

Ansdell speculates that one reason why music seems to kindle hopefulness is linked to what music does in, and with, time. Music, Ansdell observes, lifts us out of clock time and out of the other ways that we might be experiencing time in the here-and-now of the moment, in relation to things that qualify time as good or bad, pleasant or anxious.

Of course, music is only one medium that can 'lift' us out of clock time. Our experience of time is, arguably, always culturally mediated, brought to consciousness by the things that express it. If, for example, we are in the full flow of a joyous occasion time may pass quickly, if we are in pain, lying awake at night, time will pass slowly. The point is that our experience of time takes shape through the ways in is in contrast with the events and the rhythm of what is happening to us and in our environment and how these things are mediated by the meanings we attribute to them. But music has a special relationship to our temporal awareness. Music's rhythmic dimension—the ways that music organises time into patterns—makes it a particularly useful medium for re-configuring temporal experience. For example, the precise and perfectly regular beats of a metronome do not, in themselves 'package' time. A ticking metronome (or clock) does not arrange the beats in interrelated compartments (for example of accented groups of four plus four as in march music, or three plus three as in waltzing). On the other hand, when a clock chimes the hour, or the quarter hours, the ticking takes on meaning, and we begin to understand time's passing in units—hours, half hours, quarter hours, minutes. This marking of time, bunching, arranging, producing pattern and meaningful units is one of the things that music does extremely well. Music takes the mechanical beat of the metronome and, through an overlay of volume, pitch, texture, tempo, repetition, tonal relationships, tuning, timbre, rhythmic divisions, synchrony, and sequence (and of course all the social and bodily procedures and processes and situation that accompany these sonic parameters), music re-sounds (remediates) time as pattern and meaning.

This musical remediation of time can be especially powerful—and potentially transformative. Music can dramatically alter our sense of how much time has passed; it can make a long time seem short and vice versa (this point is well illustrated in the literatures on music and movement [DeNora 2000: 75–109]) and music can, often without our conscious awareness, eclipse attitudes and feelings that we had prior to engaging with music and in ways that may lead us to do things we had not intended, such as remain in a shop and even make a purchase (DeNora 2000, 2003). When we engage with, and become captivated by music, we may become *entrained* into music's parameters and drawn into emotional associations that it connotes, for us. To the extent that these things happen, we are capable of being musically transformed, re-ordered in the sense of being recalibrated, experiencing the here and now differently while immersed in a transformative medium. At times this recalibration, musically speaking, can be therapeutic; we emerge more energized, thoughtful, positive, motivated… It is any surprise, therefore, that Doctor King called for 'music therapy' when he 'felt down'?

*   *   *

To gather up what we need in order to hope (feeling motivation, for example), and then to be able to project our hopes into some kind of space, is never passive. It is, as I said already, a form of work. This is to say that hope is never simply about wishing and waiting. The act of producing hope always will have consequences. To hope is to make, however small, a *change in the present*—the actual present, not merely how we might wish to portray realities. In other words, it is to re-furbish our world with some new aspect or dimension. When we hope, we are being creative. We bring to life (projecting, infecting), imaginatively and sometimes in action, a part of the future (events, circumstances, people, states of being, places) that we may be longing for. And each new part contributes to something new, to a different way of experiencing the past, to a different set of circumstances that we step into and which become the future. These thoughts require further explanation.

The word, 're-furbished', captures how, in the act of hoping, we are also, even if minutely, fleshing out alternatives to whatever the present might currently contain. As I have discussed in Chapter 2 the philosopher Ernst Bloch considered dreaming and imagination to play a central role in any attempt to sustain an alternate vision of reality. This is because using the imagination helps to flesh out an imagined, 'better' future—it gives it content. And this is why hoping is a creative activity—it positively fleshes out its object.

The creative fleshing out of a vision is, as I shall now discuss in the remainder of this book, *causative*. It develops (changes) our awareness and our consciousness (and thus the resources we have to think and act with), individually and collectively. And in this type of development we step into a different present moment, one that becomes a kind of mini-future, that is something that is symbolically, sometimes physically, *away from* troubling features of the present. Hirokazu Miyazaki has described this process as drawing the future into the present (Miyazaki and Sweberg 2016); I would qualify this slightly (if I have understood their text correctly): I would say that the act of hoping draws the present into the (next moment) future *because* it draws an imagined future— a part of the dream—into the present. In other words, if I articulate a dream or vision of how things might be and how I hope they will become, I am adding something to the now—something new—which of course changes that now, even if infinitesimally. Once I've spoken, the dream is 'out there', whether in a social world or, as in the case of secret hoping, in my consciousness as a future possibility. The light, as it were, has subtly changed.

Through this imaginative engagement we may come to 'see things differently', or 'be calmed (or energized)' for example. And through this change, the present can be relit, or recharged (it becomes a time of possibility as opposed to a time of waiting or bearing with). In other words, the present moment gains new meaning, becomes a kind of 'poised' space, that is a specific kind of place where things could be improved and certainly a place that offers respite, even if fleetingly. We have, through the activity of hoping, established (even if projected only upon our mental space, privately) within our present lifeworld part of a dream, that is an impulse or glimmer of how and what things could *become*. This is why I consider that to hope is to exercise 'the power of imagination'.

* * *

Importantly, when we hope, we hope through resort to cultural materials. We turn to culture (as did Doctor King and Nuri) to nurture our capacity to hope, and to give shape and content to that for which we hope. At times, we appropriate cultural materials and cultural activities specifically for this purpose of refurnishing, recalibrating and respecifying present realities. Gary Ansdell quotes Louis to illustrate this point:

> When I'm playing music…the brain just goes completely blank…except there is music! And I seem to have forgotten everything…everything else goes to the back of the brain – and I become focused and I'm thinking only about music… (Ansdell 2014: 281)

Through this process, *time*, as Ansdell describes, becomes 'better'— there are 'moments of "good time"…' (ibid.) or *Kairos* (meaningful, full time as opposed to *Chronos* or regular, mechanically measured time, the externally defined time of the clock) when 'a present moment suddenly opens out and thickens' (ibid.; see also Trondalen 2016). For some people time's opening out might be experienced as 'respite' from distress. And in this sense, *altered time becomes symbolic space*, a place in which to imagine and to dream. Various forms of cultural engagement can facilitate this kind of removal from care or distress. For example, here, Thomas, confined to a wheelchair and living in a care home after experiencing a severe injury comments on the importance of fantasy life, aided by the use of his iPad:

> Thomas …says he's researching beautiful Venetian palazzos that he might live in. He suddenly says "You probably think I'm a fantasist?", and I say well sometimes we need fantasies in this life, and he smiles wistfully. He explains that the desire for a kind of fantasy life often strikes him here, confined in this place. In contrast during the next hour together we travel backwards into the reality of his past musical life where there's is a sense of solid reality in our talk….
>
> We have a conversation about weighing fantasy and imagination against so-called 'real life' at this time of his life, in his situation. Thomas describes how he still fantasising about moving to a Venetian palazzo, but now he's also looking at a cottage in a village in Cornwall. He nearly phoned the estate agent to say he'll view it. He's painfully aware that this is just fantasy, but says, "the fantasy comes very close to reality some times of the day." Telling me about the cottage leads him to tell me about how

this area of the country reminds him of a positive phase of his life when he would holiday in that part of the UK. He's aware that in his state of physical health all this is largely an illusion. He comments that people like me who have a life "out there in the world" can still have fantasies, but these are weighted down the other side by reality. But he's lost the balancing weight, and this is where fantasy starts to intrude dangerously and upsets his emotionally equilibrium. (Ansdell, Reflections on Care for Music)

Courtesy of his iPad, Thomas gains virtual mobility—he 'goes' to Venice, or Cornwall, in his imagination and through that travel he removes himself, for a while, from the otherwise unpleasant reality of where he 'really' is. In earlier work on music's role as a kind of 'asylum' (DeNora 2015 [2013]), I have spoken of the ways that going 'into' music can offer 'refuge' or haven removing us, virtually, from noxious stimuli and stressful situations, and offering entry to a private world. Here, going as it were, into a dream-world is a form of creative isolation. It offers a way of relaxing and being refreshed. It is respite and as such it can—as other researchers have described—be part of personal health-promotion strategies (Batt-Rawden 2007; Skånland 2011) and in ways that connect to the subject matter of Chapter 3. In Thomas' case, that respite and the fantasies that produce it allow Thomas what we might think of as virtual hope. Thomas returns, at times, as he describes, with difficulty, to what Alfred Schutz might call the 'paramount' reality (his situation in a care home).

It would be wrong to say that his virtual engagements with the dream of being elsewhere do not have any 'real' effects for Thomas. His dreaming not only refreshes; it is a practice that enables him to endure and remain energized and able to do what he is still able to do in constrained circumstances—to read, to think, and—vitally importantly—to have 'news'—something to talk about with others (and our dreams are indeed material for sharing). Dreaming, indulging in imagining fantasy worlds, can contribute to our ability to cope with our so-called 'real' world. Moreover, as we shall see (Chapters 4 and 5), dreaming can contribute to that world and it can produce new worlds. Thomas' fantasies were in fact a way of repopulating his world with things, and imaginary spaces where, he—*could be, better*. These dreams were by no means hermetically sealed off from Thomas' 'paramount reality'. At times of enforced confinement (including the times of 'lockdown' during the COVID pandemic), being able to discover forms of creative isolation or forms of creative 'asylum' can be vital to mental wellbeing, and the creative play within an alterative 'theatre' can have spinoff effects down the line in daily life (MacDonald et al. under review).

In my earlier work on 'music asylums', and in contrast to privately imagined, fantasy worlds, I have also considered how moments of asylum may arise from the actual furnishing or environments and habitats (and of course, as I have just described, Thomas was also furnishing his habitat with images and talk about his private fantasies of living in Venice or Cornwall). Furnishing involves the kind of projection and infection [cultural contagion] discussed in Chapter 2. It 'works on' shared spaces so as to make them more conducive to the things one dreams about and hopes for. And it does so in a manner that allows those dreams collectively to be shared and mutually elaborated—*projected* in other words—a process that is critical to collective action and activism.

This kind of 'social' furnishing involves bringing materials into a setting, scene, or situation (materials here meaning anything from references to topics of conversation, to the language employed for conversation [English or Spanish? Bokmål or Nynorsk?]). Those materials may include modes of personal attire or style, aesthetic materials more generally including the arts, physical objects and types of action (including gestures). These materials give an accent or 'feel' to the places where they are inserted and in ways can be conducive to wellbeing, not only privately but also according to how they are acknowledged, validated, and shared. (For example: 'I'm so glad they decided to paint this café pale pink, *aren't you*? Don't you just love the colour pink?' Or, 'I am happy that we can begin to speak to each other in Norwegian instead of English'.) Both the materials inserted, and the modes of calling attention to those materials, can alter perceived environments. They can speak to our senses, offer sensory enrichment and diversion, and add resources, pretexts and opportunities for action. They can induce, support, and sustain the sense of motivation, energy, coherence and identity relations. They give, in Stern's sense, vitality forms, by which Stern means, "…a

Gestalt that emerges from the theoretically separate experiences of movement, force, time, space and intention" (Stern 2010: 5) (for example, one might get the reputation for being a 'high energy' person—that is a gestalt or composite; it is composed of perhaps many things one does and how one moves).

At times our orientation and vitality form can change swiftly, for example in response to a smell on a breeze (as I write this sentence I smell lilacs in season and am momentarily diverted into channels of pleasure and memory), a whiff of someone's perfume or personal odor, a tiny accent of colour in a painting or in a room ('Oh, what beautiful flowers' or 'the part I love is that little dot of bright blue in the lower right corner'), a snatch of music overheard through an open window or recalled in memory. Through these micro-moments, glimpses and glimmers—and this is important—there is, at the very least—and perhaps only minimally but nonetheless—a change in *us*.

And if a space contains or is revamped so as to contain things that offer forms of vitality ('I'm just going to move this seat closer to the window—ah, feel that breeze and *smell the lilacs*') we are paving the way, no matter how minutely, for change outside of us. When things bring pleasure, consolation, comfort, a source of energy, confidence, or even just a bit of respite, time out, space to oneself ('I love sitting in this cozy-corner') they renew us, they show the way to new patterns of behavior, new ideas, new possibilities. Thus, the renewal that comes from cultural engagement is simultaneously a form of empowerment/enablement. It helps to rekindle imagination and thus boost the impulse to be hopeful and to engage in the activity of hoping. Renewal can come from hoping (as in when we 'catch' the contagion of hope or as in when we project into our mental or social worlds hopeful imagery or visions). And it can come from other forms of cultural activity that recharge us, fortify us *for* hoping, and help us to flesh out the dreams for which we hope. Our engagement in culture prepares us for hoping; it can move us and propel us, it can help to keep us fired up with our visions and our dreams.

As Ansdell puts it, momentary engagement with culture, for example stumbling upon something special or beautiful (to us), can create special, and sometimes epiphanic moments which nurture us because they:

...initiate a momentum beyond themselves...their epiphany is generative...We perhaps need to, then, to ask ... What is 'now' *for*? What
overall pattern of the whole do such epiphanic moments connect with
and prepare for?...Where do they move *towards*? (Ansdell 2014: 288)

One answer to Ansdell's question is, they move us into dreaming. They
awaken emotional energy (or more precisely affect, understood as a state
of physical arousal) and from there the affective impulse takes shape, gets
objectified, with a vision—and that takes shape intra-culturally and in
relation to things in the environment (DeNora 2003: 115). So, hoping,
if it is conceptualized as something more than casual wishing, and more
than strategic planning, involves feeling— becoming inspired, aroused,
emotionally engaged. There is, in other words, an aesthetic dimension to
hoping, in other words, a sensibility and an embodied transformation.
We seem to need the right emotional calibration if we are to sustain
and maintain (continue to carry) hope. Without that, there is flatness,
apathy, we are an-aesthetic, that is we feel nothing; we are emotionally
numb. Being imbued with feeling is itself a kind of empowerment as it
flows through us and quickens the pulse, the blood, the brain. And if
hope is fueled by what we find, and engage with, culturally, it therefore
becomes important to look at the cultural shape, and shaping, of hope.

4.2   Culture and Identity

Culture is stories, ideas, images, gestures, sensory things such as smells
and tastes, material practices and ways of handling things (clay, food,
a keyboard, a hammer, a needle and thread). It is meaningful and
symbolic objects such as pictures and pots and books and songs. Culture
is language and poetics. Culture offers models and categorical systems—
for example of the kinds of people we might/might not (wish to) be or
resemble. In relation to identity models, we may engage in imaginative
role taking, and this exercise is a key feature of how we gear ourselves up,
and into, hope. The music therapist Even Ruud describes how:

The musical experience is a virtual performative space where I can engage in playful and transformative identity processes, which can later be enacted in real life. (Ruud 2010: 50–51)

If hope is to be carried in all of its senses, as we have seen, its carriers need energy and focus. Part of that involves learning stances and self-images and roles through which we project ourselves as types of hopers and as located in hopeful structures and trajectories of action. As Ruud describes it, identity processes can be advanced through engagement with artistic forms.

The question of how we adjust our sense of self-identity, and the work of socially performing our self-identity, and its link to our hoping activity, and our hopes, is an important sociological matter. As a woman (and nowadays as an 'ageing' [sic] woman), I have witnessed, and, to a relatively minute extent, probably experienced discrimination, though again, I believe I have been fortunate. At the same time, I can recall that my father, a second-generation Italian-American, used to speak bitterly of the endemic prejudice he and his brothers routinely experienced growing up near Paterson in the 1920s, 1930s, prejudice that continued for a good part of his adult life.

So, the 'work' of hoping may also include work on identity politics—large and small p. Being a type of hoper, and hoping for a particular thing (types of dreams) is not independent of social, economic, political and—increasingly important as we understand the discriminatory patterns of 'lookism' (Warhurst et al. 2012; DeNora 2014)—appearance. It may be easier for some types of people to hope for some types of things and I touched on this point in all of the previous chapters. I might 'hope to go to university' but the chances of realising that hope will vary according to who I am, my economic situation and my family's educational background. I may hope to find 'love' (sic) on a dating site, or work as a newscaster, but, particularly if I am a woman, my chances may be mediated by my age, the colour of my hair, and whether I am 'too fat' (or 'too thin'). I may hope, as discussed earlier, to become President of the United States, not to be randomly stopped by the police on a regular basis, or to have a meal out in a particular restaurant, but all of these things will be mediated by other things, such as whether I have mobility (and/or the restaurant has a wheelchair ramp), the colour of my skin (and perhaps what part of New York or London I happen to be walking through), what the American political system deems to be 'leadership qualities' and many other things that are linked to the social-structural distribution of resources (economic, cultural, material), aesthetics, presumptions, prejudices. So too, I may hope to recover from disabling form of mental illness, or overcome my fear of social interaction and again, whether or not my hope will be realized may be linked to the forms of social and cultural 'capital' that I can command—the identity formats that I am able—in the eyes of others—legitimately to inhabit and sustain.

Between 2006 and 2016, Gary Ansdell and I conducted a research project on Community Music Therapy and mental health in the context of a community resource centre for mental health service users and members of the general public—SMART. We regularly observed members of the community organization SMART placing themselves inside of musical genre, styles, and songs and adopting a pose or persona:

> Robbie mentions in an off-hand way as he prepares to sing ('If I loved you') that 'I'm Billy Holiday', an affiliation that is evident in his manner of performing jazz ballads where he channels some of Holiday's delivery as his way of doing the song. (DeNora 2015 [2013]: 88)

As he sings this song, Robbie, a highly skilled musician, can be seen to *carry himself* through that song. That song, moreover, can be seen to offer him a *modus operandi* that 'carries' him, just as many of us may use what we might call, 'mood music' to carry us through tasks and situations, sustaining our motivation and identity in relation to things as diverse as doing the housework, engaging in worship, letting our hair down at a party or social event, being intimate. Putting ourselves inside of a song allows us to put ourselves inside of a model of or for a way of being. It offers parameters for interactional style. So, the song is calm, 'cool', slightly behind the beat, therefore not over-anticipating (the beat, but perhaps other things?) and the person is not over-heated, over-eager, taking its time. The properties of the former are appropriated, and get into, the properties of the latter, in and through the ways that the latter comes to appropriate the former. When we attach ourselves to media or reposition ourselves in a physical or symbolic space so as to be closer to the kinds of things that seem to lend support, we define ourselves and through that definition we can become poised to act in certain ways, with capacities of specific kinds and ready to expend energy in certain ways—as a protestor, a person of faith, a type of worker, a charismatic speaker, a fighter, a person who enjoys mental health, a lover.

So too, the cultural geography of buildings and organisations can be studied in terms of how, for different participants, different features of a space may afford (allow for the appropriation of) not only different moods, levels of energy or attitudes but potential roles or identity pathways that individuals might entertain as a part of their social 'career' (the roles they play over time) within a scene, setting, organization or program. Within the SMART café, for example, many members of the group had favourite places to sit when taking part in the musical activities—closer or further away from the piano, in a corner, front and centre, or near to the outer door. Within a care home, to give another example, we have noticed that people sometimes have favourite spots in a communal lounge—a highly valued special chair or corner for example.

In a hospital where a program of installing art work in corridors and public rooms has been established, a patient or visitor may find themselves stopping before the same picture time after time, in a way establishing a relationship with that image, and in ways that may make that part of the building feel more—hospitable—and more personal. That hospitality involves refreshment through sensory enrichment and perhaps therefore renewed energy for the next 'phase' of rehabilitation. It may also involve, as Ruud spoke of in the quote above, an opportunity to engage in identity-play, imaginatively projecting oneself into a depicted scene ('imagine being able to walk through this garden') or finding that it prompts memories of where one has been ('that is a photograph of Venice—and I have been there'), who one therefore is and how one can be known to others.

In their study of a Norwegian prison soundscape, Hjørnevik and Waage (2018) describe a similar process. They quote an inmate who recounts how a particular room seemed to offer a chance to adopt an imaginary identity:

You have to go and hang out in the music room. I like to go there. I can't play, but it makes me feel like a musician. (Hjørnevik and Waage 2018: 7)

As Hjørnevik and Waage observe, these hypothetical identity moves may lead the person from 'feeling like' a musician to beginning actively to become one. And in that becoming, there is then all the more reason to hope. Identity development gives hope further justification.

4.3   If Hope Is an Anchor, How Is Hope Itself Anchored?

Some years ago, the cultural sociologist Ann Swidler has developed the concept of cultural anchor which is helpful for understanding what is happening in these two scenarios. 'The biggest unanswered question in the sociology of culture," Swidler has suggested, 'is whether and how some cultural elements control, anchor, or organize others' (2001: 206). In my opinion, that question has yet to be fully addressed.

Swidler describes how action of any kind rests upon often entirely unnoticed or 'silent' practices that (her term) 'anchor' action and emotion. We are 'anchored' when we act in response to felt sense of reality, a sense of situation to which we then align or way of being, moving, talking, valuing. As I understand this idea, I see it connecting to, or complementing, Stern's notion of 'forms of vitality' described above. But with a twist: the ideas of silent practices and cultural anchors draw Stern's idea of vitality forms onto a sociological grounding, reconceptualising vitality forms as taking shape in relation to, or being anchored in, social contexts and social relations.

For example, I may respond to music in an embodied, emotional way (my movements may be slowed and calmed, or quickened and agitated). That response can then inform both what I say (the topic of my speech) and how I say it (in a gentler, softer manner or in a more urgent and strident tone). And this speech style will be part of the general tenor of my energy and orientation to what comes to be positioned in the forefront of my consciousness. Aesthetic media quicken and empower us emotionally and often if not always, as we saw in the example of Martin Luther King Jr and his need for gospel music. we know what, aesthetically, we need in order to remain focused, purposeful, and hopeful. Aesthetic media are in other words anchors and they can anchor hope (itself understood as an anchor) by helping to—sustain the hoper's mood and energy.

Anchors, in Swidler's sense, apply equally to collective action and it is here that it is possible to connect the earlier discussion of projection— the symbolic furnishing of social, cognitive and emotional space (recall again from Chapter 2, Todd Gitlin's comment that, in the SDS, they looked to Bob Dylan's music to see, 'where he was taking us next')— with a focus on culture's importance to keeping the hoper faithful to her or his dream. Cultural media can also anchor future action traectories, that is, they can give perceptions of a situation a tilt and thereby cue particular responses, action trajectories, stances, attitudes, and ways of behaving toward people or events. So, for example, Skånland and Trondalen (2014) have described how, after the 2011 terror attack on in Oslo, Norway, many people turned to familiar, hopeful music as a way of processing grief, but also as a way of reaffirming a hopeful belief in humankind that is, a hope that these values would be affirmed through future events. They were using music, in other words, to anchor or hold and thus prefigure or sketch out a take on future lines of conduct and orientation, actively shaping the arc of present to future and thus partially crafting, providing the scaffolding for, future scenarios.

4.4 Metaphors and Forms as Anchors

In an interview for our mental health project, Ella tells Gary that her experience of developing, and moving away from her mental health identity is:

> ...a bit like a plant...it's under the earth...you've sown a seed in the ground...and it's germinating...but you've no idea what's going on there, because it's invisible. But once that shoot comes up through the earth, you can begin to see things visibly growing...so if you take that year...in the last year...and you consider that I'm a little shoot [both laugh] and

I've actually appeared, visibly…and I'm developing a bit here and there with a bit of water and a little bit of sunshine, you know…. (Ansdell and DeNora 2016: 115)

Ella's talk reveals the anchoring metaphor—she is a little shoot that is growing. And in and through the vortex of how she speaks about it, she is growing it (and growing herself). Indeed, the 'source domain'—the image of the seedling—comes ready made with its own set of temporal stages (seed in the dark earth, a tiny shoot when it germinates, its development and expansion as it is nurtured) and these features help to drive her health narrative forward. This literary structure not only formulates events of 'the last year'. It also formulates Ella's consciousness—the categories and items that it foregrounds—the idea of growth, of light and darkness ('under the earth' versus 'sunshine'), the idea of being cultivated ('a bit of water')—become categories foregrounded—they are *projected* into—in Ella's consciousness as well. In their study of health narratives, Bonde et al. and contributing authors have described the importance—and performative importance—of metaphors, narrative and poetics in accounts of self in recovery and in relation to illness (Bonde et al. 2013). Key within this work is the focus on positioning, on foregrounding and backgrounding in stories that are put together and told.

To speak about the foregrounding and backgrounding of consciousness is to point to how any 'telling about', recounting, narrating and—in general—talking about where one is or might be able to go in future— is performative. It calls out and points to a direction that occupies the mind (is 'contagious'). And it blocks out rival possibilities (for example a rival narrative about remaining ill, or 'under the earth' and 'failing to sprout'). In a sense, this arrangement of consciousness is what Viktor Frankl meant by 'psychohygeine', as discussed in Chapter 3 (Frankl 2004). Important here is that this narrative was produced for and within a particular situation (one might suggest that it would be 'only polite' to tell the music therapist that what he was doing was 'helping'). But—the situation of telling itself fed back into how Ella was coming to see herself. (We might all be familiar with how, once we say, 'I think I'm getting better' or 'I think I see some signs for hope' we actually become the thing we thought we were merely describing—we become that little bit

stronger and more able—language, is quite literally, power and empow-
ering in these cases and very much part of the social ritual that is capable
of producing a placebo effect or a cultural immunogen.)

The point is that cultural forms and materials organise perception
(DeNora 2014). They call our attention to new and different features
of reality and in ways that can recalibrate our energy levels, moods, and
capacity for action. We may be infused with energy and we may find,
in cultural materials, models and exemplars for thinking, feeling, and
acting. To return to a musical example, consider the role of song-writing
in relation to recovery (from trauma, from mental illness) and how—
whether collaborative or sole-authored—the writing of a song offers a
remediation of past troubles, a way of coming to terms with those troubles, and a way of thinking past them and into the or 'a' future. Indeed,
in this respect it is possible to speak, following Paulo Jedlowski (2015:
126) of 'memories of the future' and in particular to consider how 'horizons of expectation' are mapped out as memories of what one might
hope to accomplish. And that future, as Arjun Appadurai has put it,
'is shot through with affect and with sensation' (2013: 287). Our envisioning, projected forward through the models and momentum afforded
by cultural forms sketches outlines of 'the' future and pulls us into
identities and actions whereby we simultaneously occupy present and
future.

The work of music therapist Randi Rolvsjord (2016), whose practice
includes collaborative songwriting helps to illustrate these last points.
Rolvsjord describes her perspective as 'resource oriented' by which
she means that it is, '...strongly connected to empowerment philosophy...' and seeks to 'amplify strengths rather than mend weaknesses'
to 'recognise competences', to 'nurture and develop the resources of
clients through musical interactions and collaborations' and to, 'focus
on musical resources and music as resource' (Rolvsjord 2005: 99). Co-
creating songs with a client allows for the narrative and musical choices to
be negotiated and in ways that may give a significant tilt to previous experience, in ways that redefine situations, identities and events and through
this—empower (and give rise for future hope).

For example, Rolvjord describes one client, Emma, who had experienced childhood abuse. She came to a session with a poem, to be set to

music. It was entitled, 'Father's Crime' and described how 'father's hand stole your soul and made the world around you so cold' (ibid.). Rolvsjord describes how:

> In the days following the session I created a song out of the poem and presented this to her in the following session....Constructing a melody implies that you involve yourself emotionally, and the melody will express some of your own feelings connected to the lyrics. It so happened in this song there was a discrepancy between the musical expression of the song which I had created and Emma's emotions and anticipations of the musical effect. I had created her song within a rock 'n' roll genre and when she listened to the song for the first time she was surprised that I had created such an angry song out of her sad lyrics. I told her that I was feeling very angry about men doing such things to their children but that we could change the song, if she wanted it to be a more sad song. She then replied, 'can you make it angrier'?...
>
> What we can learn here is that the discrepancy between my song creation and her emotions connected to the poem provided for her a new emotional experience...to give her anger an allowable expression through music. (Rolvjord 2005: 105–106)

Rolvsjord describes how this emotional shift came to provide affordances, or resources that could be used by Emma to continue to process events in her past and—key in relation to being prepared emotionally to hope—to enable her to take a new, and more empowered stance toward the future, to be empowered, in other words for what would come later, and her role in hoping for/helping to realising change (ibid.: 114). Music therapist Brynjulf Stige speaks of this process in terms of the Norwegian word, 'trivsel' which (to my knowledge) literally translates as 'wellbeing' but which, according to Stige also emphasizes the importance of 'focusing on the strengths of individuals and groups' (Stige 2004: 92). It is here where we begin to see how hope's development can be advanced through careful collaboration (i.e., collaborative practice that is full of care), and also where we see how hope is connected reflexively—causing and caused—by the incremental and often slow, micro-accumulation of resources that effect changes not only in what is hoped for but in the person who hopes.

4.5 'Ways of Happening' in Poetry and Music

It is worth taking stock at this point—what is it, in all of the examples so far considered, that cultural materials, and cultural engagement can do as part of a project of anchoring and elaborating activities of hoping? I suggest that culture offers inspiration, identity stances, energy, imagery that can furnish a dream (what hope can look or feel like) and a sense of coherence and control. That sense of control is *at once* virtual (we are perhaps not 'really' in control of the circumstances that we wish would change) and real (we can be in control of how we engage with cultural materials which offer us a space and time within which to be 'in control'). It is for all these reasons that I said, at the start of Chapter 2, that I could not accept that hoping and dreaming are distinct or that dreaming is irrational (on the latter, see Chapter 5). Culture fuels dreaming and as such provides materials for crafting, if not how things happen, how we experience those things and thus how they are, for us, real in their consequences. The case of poetry and its mediation of the experience of cancer provides a case in point.

In Iain Twiddy's (2015) study of cancer poetry, Twiddy describes how the writer Jane Yolen wrote a sonnet every day while her husband was being treated for cancer (Yolen 2003), 'both as a mark of devotion and as a means of psychological control over certain physical forms, but that control is never more than temporary' (2015: 23). Form, Twiddy, suggests, can offer reassurance ('to know and understand what is happening even if—or especially if—it is distressing' [p. 26]) and in this way (akin to the discussion in Chapter 3 of Hilbert and his study of when a source of pain comes to be identified), form can offer the comfort of social connection, even if only with form itself (the completion of a sonnet for example exhibits craft and control and it produces a new meaningful object that can re-furbish mental and symbolic space). So, the making of a new cultural object helps to produce a form of hope— the hope of retaining meaning and of holding on to, carrying, control. It is worth recalling what the philosopher Vico once said—that no knowledge was real to him unless he had 'made it himself'. Poetry is a way of 'making' knowledge—indeed, the now archaic meaning of the term 'maker' was 'poet'. So, for example, when Yolen wrote:

> We go then, hand in hand, into the deep
>   Each day a visit to the blank machines
>   Those promises we mean to keep
>   By these mechanicals or other means. (Yolen 2003: 1)

she can be seen to be redeeming a distressing situation by making a connection between (a) the mutual endurance of a period of radiation treatment (for her husband's brain tumour) with (b) the couple's forty-year history. Semiotically, through this link, the poem shifts the meaning of the X-ray machine. The machine is translated from alien and frightening object to symbol of marital commitment. It is, in other words, poetically captured and it then works as a foil to reveal the couple's devotion (to themselves, to others) and allows Yolen to say that their promises, or vows, can stand 'by these mechanicals or other means'. So, relationally, the spectre of death, the impersonal machines (which control the tumour at the price of destroying the teeth), the strangeness of cancer, *are connected to and lodged within* the sonnet structure (a highly controlled form) and its imagery—the invocation of vows made 'in sickness and in health' (that phrase is part of the subtitle of her book, *The Radiation Sonnets*), the idea of going 'hand in hand' into whatever might arise, including the machines. So, Yolen's work, the sonnet, remediates the otherwise frightening and anomic situation of cancer treatment. That remediation also re-specifies, or rather reclaims, *identity* and mutual identity—the couple's strength is renewed and redeemed in and through the poetic form and they can carry themselves and their hope for continued intimacy and—possibly—life. By producing a poetic, aesthetic medium that reconfigures experience, it is possible to—carry on and carry on hoping.

Here one might argue that the locating of a cultural medium, and the casting of experience within that medium, allows knowledge to be forged in ways that can make sense—at least to us (Vico on making knowledge himself). And that making lends a sense of being in control, of being able to have an effect on how things (meanings, the aesthetic environment) are; the process of production thus may generate knowledge about what to hope for—that is, what is 'reasonable' to hope for, when, where—and with whom. And it empowers—because of doing it we feel stronger, more capable of expression and of action, and with more ideas about what can be done. This theme will be developed in Chapter 5.

Locating resources for hope's imaginary, that is for ways of stoking and fleshing out the dream that is being carried, can be understood as the reverse of 'projecting'. It is a form of introjecting, by which I mean adopting ideas, images, stances, orientations, visions, metaphors, materials, attaching oneself to these things in ways that structure our approach the world, what we notice, the aesthetic responses we have to what we encounter.

Music therapist Brynjulf Stige has described this process as one that creates agency through, 'internalization and creative use of cultural artifacts in social contexts' (2002: 35). I shall speak of this as 'introjection' but in a sense that is very different from the psychoanalytic sense of that term where it is associated with internalizing voices of authority unduly. Here, introjection is about the appropriation of resources that can help and that can promote the ability to carry the dream. So, as in the case of poetic forms, materials are offered for introjection which in turn affect how we respond to the things that are their topics (how we respond, for example, to X-ray machines). In relation to cancer poetry, for example, there are genre, such as the elegy and the elegiac voice, with its seasonal mood of autumn or winter, its focus on the act of mourning, that can prime or help to condition our stances and attitudes toward situation and circumstance. Twiddy outlines how, in the face of loss or impending loss, energies may be recast through form in ways that offer outlets for emotion and that channel those emotions, projecting into the present new forms of self-understanding and—new forms of acting. Twiddy quotes Donald Hall, speaking to his dead wife in a letter poem in a way that describes how he is not 'separating from his wife, but being overtaken by her' (2015: 33):

> In daydream I spend afternoons
> Digging around your peonies

To feed them my grandfather's fifty-year-old cow manure.
Next week maybe I'll menstruate.

Poetry, Twiddy reminds us with reference to Seamus Heaney, 'artic-ulates "the imagination pressing back against the pressure of reality"' (2015: 161). Ultimately, Twiddy concludes, poetry is much more than comfort in the face of adversity, and more than control through casting of aesthetic form. It offers an alternate way of being that can:

> ...sound more beautifully, and for now more powerfully, than the repeating spheres of cancer, regardless of whether or not a sufferer survives. It may also demonstrate how, in light of the planetary scale of cancer, poetry can be, in its forms and rhythms and harmonies, a measure of the force that moves the sun and the other stars. (2015: 198)

Which is to say that poetry (one could say the same for music, painting, and many other cultural practices that involve and invoke sensory modal-ities) *is* a 'world' that is real in its consequences because it is 'a measure' (Twiddy's words) of that world. So just as music can capture time and give it meaning—as interval, as passage (as discussed earlier through Ansdell's discussion of music therapy and hope), poetry can capture meaning and become, in W. H. Auden's sense, 'a way of happening' (Auden 1940, 'In Memory of W. B. Yeats'). More prosaically, this means that, in entering the poetic world, the 'reality' at time 1, of suffering, is transcended. In that transcendence, people, whether real or imagined, can be brought together and in ways that may make a difference to how, privately and together they experience any given reality down the line, at time 2.

* * *

To carry a dream involves a great deal of activity. It involves locating a dream in imagery or aesthetic media, and it involves carrying the dream which in turn involves different forms of support (and transport, and not always under, as it were, 'our own steam'), it involves adapting a dream to changing circumstances. It involves producing ourselves and others as ready to carry a dream—emotionally prepared, calibrated, and energized. And it involves modifying our understandings of ourselves and our circumstances as we approximate the things for which we hope.

In her exploration of how song-writing was a method for overcoming severe Post Traumatic Stress Disorder, Georgina Lewis describes how she was involved in this type of process:

> Performing trauma in music allows the collision of a haunting beauty with pain—the communication perhaps of a thread of hope within the hurt. My song "The River" […] communicated my wish to die, something that is especially difficult to do in the spoken word, but the song affords the entwined intimacy of singing with the vulnerability of my own life. Whilst the words are desperately sad, the piano has some stunning chords and melody lines. I knew then if I could write something beautiful then I could keep living—music provided me the chance to communicate to myself that whilst I was in pain, and had a right to feel and express it, I still had life in me. In the song, I lived safely within the paradox of expressing severe pain whilst realising my will to live. (Lewis 2017: 6)

Here, the song became a lens through which Lewis could, as it were, see herself, and thus resources for living with, and moving away from, pain. Lewis describes how (her) pain was reformatted in music and through music—the source, quality and quantity of pain, in this remediation was, we might say, introjected (that is, her sense of herself in pain, and her sense of her pain) was altered in relation to new ways of perceiving, and remembering, pain. New ways of focusing, noticing and remarking on 'what happened' and 'how I feel' reorganized the reality of the pain and with it the real potentiality of where Lewis might go over time ('the thread of hope within the hurt'). Cultural forms, one might say, thus re/enact, in 'magic realist' ways our experience of the past, ourselves, the future; the draw out of us new forms of knowledge and new capabilities.

By magic realist I mean that cultural materials—poetic or musical forms are the examples I have used so far—are resources for transcendence, for moving beyond pre-set realities. They recast realities and, in giving things new forms (some, more, different, form), engaging with cultural materials, whether as reader, listener, composer or writer, can enhance the person who engages—enhance their capacity, sense of empowerment and ability or energy with which to hope. In introjecting imagery, metaphors, media, in furnishing spaces with resources conducive to wellbeing or spiritual contentment or inspiration or glimpses of another universe, we are creating new vistas, new capacities and new imaginary forms of acting—scenarios, yes, but also new cognitive skills. We are quickening our imagination and in ways that both allow us to live with difficult circumstances and work out new angles on what we might do to effect change (Back's 'attention to the present' as discussed in Chapter 2). This is an on-going process and one in which we engage in a two-directional adjustment of our dream (expanding, contracting our imagined horizons) and our carrying activities in light of what happens moment to moment.

The example just considered from Lewis highlights how the 'real' and the 'magical' interleave with current interdisciplinary understandings of pain perception and pain management, and in ways that produce 'hard' or 'physiological' changes in pain. It also underlines the importance of creative activity to mental health (Ansdell and DeNora 2016). I have already considered the co-called 'placebo effect' and examined the theories of why it seems that 'placebos' may work as well, if not better than traditional treatments and procedures. The point then is that there is a place for culture in healthcare, and in what we might speak of here as public health (Fancourt and Finn 2019) and that place needs to recognize culture as causative, as an active ingredient even in matters physiological. So, participation in culture can keep us strong and 'able' to dream, to plan, to act and to be alert to the present so that we know when as it were the time for action arrives. To hope requires and sustains emotional power. And the emotional power *to* hope comes from the ways that we imbibe and introject cultural forms and resources which in turn give form and content to our agency as those who have hope. The study of hope is also the study of where realities come from, and thus, the study of the continual exchange between what counts as reality and fantasy.

4.6   Fantasy Versus Reality?

In a study that examines how children fantasise and hope in relation to the illness of a parent (and the likelihood that they will lose a parent), Ditte Alexandra Winther-Lindqvist explores how these children's imaginings, 'often take the form of hope' (2017: 152). In one—deceptively simple—sentence, Winther-Lindqvist explains why the interrelationship between hope and dreaming (imagination) is of utmost importance:

> I recognize hope as a form of imaginative activity and practice, because hope is formed in light of an uncertain future, and rests upon imagined scenarios of what could be. (2017: 152)

As I understand her words, Winther-Lindqvist envisions hope as a mixture of fantasy and practice—as activity. She then develops a grounded understanding of this mixture through her analysis of her interviews with children. Her work taps and builds upon the work of developmental psychologist Lev Vygotsky's theory of imagination (Vygotsky 2004). Key to her exploration of imagination, is the distinction between imagination and its products, fantasy—that is what is imagined. Hoping, she argues, serves as, 'an imaginary backdrop, against which events and tasks, moods and impressions are experienced and evaluated and thus the fantasies involved in hoping become constitutive for experience' (ibid.). Imaginative play, it would seem, is an important part of the adult business of hoping. Imaginative play scaffolds hope, allowing for movement from the present to the future—which resonates with Vygotsky's idea of the zone of proximal development (Vygotsky 1978).

To play involves, as Sutton Smith has suggested, 'acting out one's capacity for the future' (quoted in DeNora 2015 [2013]: 42), and perhaps as such, to be engaged in play is to be involved in an activity that is antithetical to depression—it is, quintessentially creative and perhaps should be declared a human right. This is why the environments in which we operate are often environments that we work on, modifying, adapting, refurnishing or else retreating from distressing situations into daydream, novels, films, games, or music via headphones or, if cultural resources are not available, ultimately, psychic withdrawal.

Winther-Lindqvist views hope, with its fantasies, as a form of protection against despair (a point to which I return in Chapter 5). This point is elaborated by Sarah H. Awed, in a study of the letters written by political prisoners in Egypt, post 2011. Awed suggests that letters offer their writers a form of 'aesthetic resistance to confinement and authority' (2017: 267). Imagination, she argues, is the capacity to distance oneself from the here-and-now in order to return to it with new possibilities' (ibid.). Following Goethe (to whom I return on Chapter 5), Awed advances a perspective that fantasy and imagination complement, rather than oppose, scientific rationality:

> Individuals use aesthetic tools in their environment for reflection, intuition and everyday resistance to what they perceive as threatening (Teo 2015). Aesthetics therefore opens the horizon of our imagination to deal with the possible, the impossible, the ideal, and the implausible, allowing us to challenge the status quo.

Following Winther-Lindqvist and Awed, we might conclude that not only is imagination integral to the activity of hoping, but that it is integral to the more pragmatic side of hoping as well ('opens the horizons of our imagination to deal…') and I will develop this thought in Chapter 5. That pragmatism involves the pursuit of a goal and it involves methods and techniques. Imagination, in other words, can be understood to be part of any rational effort to effect change, not only insofar as it stokes hope's motivation but, more radically, because it sharpens and recharges cognition. Imaginatively reworking the world, going into the dream, we return to a world that is not quite the same as the one we left. It is not the same because we are not the same, that is our perceptual apparatus has been recharged in ways that may equip us to think, feel, and perceive things differently, that is, we have gained resourcefulness as well as motivation to continue in pursuit of something different in the future. There is, in other words, a mutual constitution of the here-and-now and the future in terms of our relationship to the what passes as reality.

We saw this point exemplified in the song-writing activities of Georgina and Emma who reconstituted past situations, and therefore their current capabilities, by recasting these things in song, and as we saw in the examples of cancer poetry and its genre, voices and metaphors. It is precisely this that the music therapist Even Ruud is pointing to when he says that music, whether through listening, through visualisation exercises set to music, or through participation in live music or music therapy, offers 'possibilities for action' (2008) in the sense that it can be the activating agent for the individual's development of new ideas, new senses of self-identity and new 'scripts' or action scenarios, all of which are developed in relation to feelings and to imaginative engagement. Imagination, in short, 'creates real feelings' (Winther-Lindqvist 2017: 154).

We are now at a place where the distinction between the virtual, or culturally mediated, and the real, can be dispensed with. This is the place where dreams are integral even to the most pragmatic or rational forms of hoping, and where things that are imagined may be 'real in their consequences' (DeNora 2014). We have arrived at a place where it is meaningful, indeed, 'scientific' to speak of an 'intelligence of feeling' (Witkin 1974) or way of knowing that elides conscious, propositional awareness but involves the body, mood, emotion and the senses.

In her study of body-memory, Anna Lisa Tota (2016), describes how cultural forms—dance forms specifically—can draw out things about us that we might not have known we could do, or know. A movement, a particular figure, a ritual—all of these may 'dance the past' to us in ways that may reveal (transform?) suppressed or forgotten memories—and transform them/us. So too, Tota describes how traumatic experiences can be transformed when such pasts become visible—they can then pass, be allowed to go, and in those moments, they are no longer a burden but are transformed into, 'a resource, into a stabilizing anchor for the person's future life' (2016: 470). The philosopher J. J. Godfrey suggested that hope, 'is somehow prehensile, enabling a person to in some sense know what would, without hope, be beyond that person's grasp' (1987: xi). By this logic, hoping, if it involves imaginative translations, re-castings of the past and the present, can be understood to be both grounded on, and generating, emotional intelligence—hope is the ability to imagine novel possibilities and to be attentive to the present and its offering of opportunities to put hope into action. What, then, can't hope do?

References

Ansdell, G. (2014). *How Music Helps: In Music Therapy and Everyday Life*. London: Routledge.

Ansdell, G., & DeNora, T. (2016). *Musical Pathways in Recovery: Community Music Therapy and Mental Wellbeing*. London: Routledge.

Appadurai, A. (2013). *The Future as Cultural Fact: Essays on the Global Condition*. London: Verso.

Auden, W. H. (1940). *Another Time*. London: Random House.

Awed, S. H. (2017). 'We Are Not Free, Admit It…But We Cling Onto Tomorrow': Imagination as a Tool for Coping in Disempowering Situations. In B. Wagoner, I. Bresco de Luna, & S. Awad (Eds.), *The Psychology of Imagination: History, Theory and New Research Horizons* (pp. 267–281). Charlotte, NC: Information Age Publishing Inc.

Batt-Rawden, K. B. (2007). Music as a Transfer of Faith: Towards Recovery and Healing. *Journal of Research in Nursing, 12*(1), 87–99.

Bonde, L. O., Ruud, E., Strand Skånland, M., & Trondalen, G. (Eds.). (2013). *Musical Life Stories: Narratives on Health Musicking*. Oslo: Norges Musikkhøgskole Publikasjoner.

DeNora, T. (2000). *Music in Everyday Life*. Cambridge: Cambridge University Press.

DeNora, T. (2003). *After Adorno: Rethinking Music Sociology*. Cambridge: Cambridge University Press.

DeNora, T. (2014). *Making Sense of Reality: Culture and Perception in Everyday Life*. London: Sage.

DeNora, T. (2015 [2013]). *Music Asylums: Wellbeing Through Music in Everyday Life*. London: Routledge.

Eyerman, R., & Jameson, A. (1998). *Music and Social Movements*. Cambridge: Cambridge University Press.

Fancourt, D., & Finn, S. (2019). *What Is the Evidence on the Role of the Arts in Improving Health and Well-being?* Copenhagen: World Health Organisation.

Frankl, V. E. (2004 [1946]). *Man's Search for Meaning*. London: Ebury.

Godfrey, J. (1987). *A Philosophy of Human Hope*. Dordrecht, Boston and Lancaster: Martinus Nijhoff Publishers.

Hjørnevik, K., & Waage, L. (2018). The Prison as a Therapeutic Music Scene: Exploring Musical Identities in Music Therapy and Everyday Life in a Prison Setting. *Punishment and Society, 21*(4), 454–472.

Jedlowski, P. (2015). Memories of the Future. In A. L. Tota and T. Hagen (Eds.), *Routledge International Handbook of Memory Studies* (pp. 121–30). London: Routledge.

Lewis, G. (2017). "Let Your Secrets Sing Out": An Auto- Ethnographic Analysis on How Music Can Afford Recovery From Child Abuse. *Voices, 17*(2), n.p. Retrieved on March 21, 2020 from https://voices.no/index.php/voices/article/view/2346.

McKesson, D. (2017). *On the Other Side of Freedom: The Case for Hope.* Penguin Books.

Miyazaki, H., & Sweberg, R. (Eds.). (2016). *The Economy of Hope.* Philadelphia: University of Pennsylvania Press.

Rolvsjord, R. (2005). Collaborations on Songwriting with Clients with Mental Health Problems. In F. Baker & T. Wigram (Eds.), *Songwriting: Methods, Techniques and Clinical Applications for Music Therapy Clinicians, Educators and Students* (pp. 97–115). London: Jessica Kingsley.

Rolvsjord, T. (2016). *Resource-Oriented Music Therapy in Mental Health Care.* Gilsum, NH: Barcelona Publishers.

Ruud, E. (2008). Music in Therapy: Increasing Possibilities for Action. *Music and Arts in Action, 1*(1), 46–60.

Ruud, E. (2010). *Music Therapy: A Perspective from the Humanities.* Gilsum, NH: Barcelona Publishers.

Skånland, M. S. (2011). Use of Mp3-players as Coping Resource. *Music and Arts in Action, 3*(2), 15–33.

Skånland, M. S., & Trondalen, G. (2014). Music and Grief: Norway After 22 July, 2011. *Voices: A World Forum for Music Therapy, 14*(2). Retrieved on April 16, 2020 from https://voices.no/index.php/voices/article/view/2230.

Stern, D. N. (2010). *Forms of Vitality: Exploring Dynamic Experience in Psychology and the Arts.* Oxford: Oxford University Press.

Stige, B. (2002). *Culture-Centered Music Therapy.* Gilsum, NH: Barcelona Publishers.

Stige, B. (2004). Community Music Therapy: Culture, Care and Welfare. In M. Pavlicevic & G. Ansdell (Eds.), *Community Music Therapy* (pp. 91–113). London: Jessica Kingsley Publishers.

Swidler, A. (2001). What Anchors Cultural Practices? In T. Schatzki, K. K. Cetina, & E. von Savigny (Eds.), *The Practice Turn in Social Theory* (pp. 74–92). London: Routledge.

Tota, A. L. (2016). Dancing the Present: Body Memory and Quantum Field Theory. In A. L. Tota & T. Hagen (Eds.), *Routledge International Handbook of Memory Studies* (pp. 458–472). London: Routledge.

Trondalen, G. (2016). *Relational Music Therapy: An Intersubjective Perspective.* Dallas, TX: Barcelona Publishers.

Twiddy, I. (2015). *Cancer Poetry.* Basingstoke: Palgrave Macmillan.

Vygotsky, L. S. (1978). Mind in Society: The Development of Higher Psychological Processes. In M. Cole, V. John-Steiner, S. Scribner, & E. Souberman (Eds.), Cambridge, MA: Harvard University Press.

Vygotsky, L. (2004). Imagination and Creativity in Childhood. *Journal of Russian and East European Psychology, 42*(1), 7–97.

Warhurst, C., van den Broek, D., Hall, R., & Nickson, D. (2012). Great Expectations: Gender, Looks and Lookism at Work. *International Journal of Work, Organisation, and Emotion, 5*(1), 72–90.

Winther-Lindqvist, D. A. (2017). Hope as Fantasy: An Existential Phenomenology of Hoping in Light of Parental Illness. In B. Wagoner, I. Bresco de Luna, & S. Awad (Eds.), *The Psychology of Imagination: History, Theory and New Research Horizons.* Charlotte, NC: Information Age Publishing Inc.

Witkin, R. W. (1974). *The Intelligence of Feeling.* Portsmouth, NH: Heinemann Educational Publishers.

Yolen, J. (2003). The Radiation Sonnets: For My Love, in Sickness and in Health. *Family & Community Health, 29*(1), 68.

Younge, G. (2013). *The Speech: The Story Behind Martin Luther King's Dream.* Chicago: Haymarket Books.

5

Social Hope

Understanding hope as an activity means understanding that hope takes shape in relation to many things outside of individuals. It means, as I have discussed in Chapter 2, understanding hope in terms of the inter-connected practices of 'carrying' physical and symbolic objects through bringing, protecting, projecting, infecting and realising. It means, as discussed in Chapter 3, understanding hope a cultural immunogen, that is, practices by which we extend ourselves and our communities, poten-tially enhancing resistance to physical and social pathogens. And it means understanding as discussed in Chapter 4, how individuals engage in activities of introjecting or internalizing media and materials that can be found in the cultural environment in ways that enhance the basis for, and give shape to, the present moment and thus, to hope and its sustainability.

Hope is something we produce; we make hope in relation to each other and in relation to culture and this production highlights how hope is always a collective, social project even when the person who hopes may be in isolation or captivity. It is social for the reasons just described, namely that it is produced in relation to many things that lie outside of individuals. And it is social because, in hoping, we are

© The Author(s), under exclusive license to Springer Nature
Switzerland AG 2021
T. DeNora, *Hope*,
https://doi.org/10.1007/978-3-030-69870-6_5

producing ourselves as types of actors, specifically as actors prepared to act in the present and future and in opportunistic ways oriented to change. Martin Luther King Junior once spoke of how it was possible to 'hew…a stone of hope' from the 'mountain of despair'. Of interest here, is how this 'hewing' of opportunities in and over time, in whatever ways may become available, gets done and in this final chapter the metaphor of the mountain will be brought into view.

Hoping can, I will now suggest, be understood as part of our potential social agency and thus as part of empowerment. At the same time, it is important not to exaggerate what hope can (or cannot) do. I suggest that consideration of these questions requires an even closer look at what it means to dream and what—in a real and practical sense—dreaming is and what it does. If hope involves carrying a dream, then what can't hope do? The wording of this question is deliberately ambiguous. It asks, simultaneously, what might be the things that hope *cannot* do? And it asks, whatever is there that can hope cannot do?

5.1   What Can't Hope Do?

We have seen how hope can be captured and linked to organizational and institutional agendas ('have hope: take this medicine; vote for this politician/party'), how hope can be trivialized as positivity and blithe optimism ('it will all be ok, something will turn up'). We have seen how some forms of hoping can deflect our attention from what ought to be shared, practical projects involving adaptations and generous alterations in shared plans or aims (a mind-set that says, 'this person cannot [walk, speak, remember…] so they cannot join us for this activity today but *hopefully* someday a cure will be found and they will be with us again', as opposed to a mind-set that says, 'let's think about how we can find a way that will let them join even if a cure cannot be found'). And we have seen how hope can be a torment keeping us sometimes unrealistically bound into anticipating what not only will never arrive but what might be impossible.

As a stand-alone activity, hope is unlikely to fix a broken leg, cure cancer, address racism or global poverty, or make roses bloom in

November in Norway. To believe that hope, on its own, can make these things happen is not only misguided; it inculcates passivity. It distracts us from what otherwise might be done (such as setting a bone, making the most of the time one has, effecting concrete cultural and economic change, or admiring the shapes of the shrubs when denuded of flowers, fruit and leaves, but covered in snow). Hope, in other words, not only needs to be appropriate to what can, realistically be hoped for; it needs to be diagnostic and opportunistic; active; alert to what can be done to advance or realise the dream, even if in miniscule increments. And thinking about the miniscule highlights the place where the paradox of dreaming becomes clear; it reminds us that the divide between dream and reality is blurry since dreaming is a part of what produces empowered action and action's effects in the world.

Dreaming is action because it can kindle a sense of empowerment which, even when dreaming of roses out of doors in November (a probably futile hope) can be of benefit. This benefit derives from the ways that we are or feel more 'whole' when we feel closer to things we believe in and deem meaningful, irrespective of their realism (whether judged by ourselves or by others). So, for example, even if it seems likely that one will not 'escape' from a predicament or situation (incurable illness; captivity; natural disaster; pandemic), some forms of hoping can be helpful. Hoping can help because, as discussed in Chapter 3 in relation to the placebo effect, it can deflect our attention from things that are distressing and as such, it can assist us to sustain a sense of coherence in troubled times in ways that alleviate distress and thus perhaps be more open and prepared to act when opportunities arise. Under less duress, less stressed, we may become more resourceful and perhaps even discover methods of addressing, or at least enduring, negative circumstances.

But beyond this palliative function, I suggest that hoping, even impossible hoping, may contribute significantly to change, albeit to varying degrees. This transformative capacity of hoping is linked to the degree to which dreaming, and carrying dreams, in the sense of being 'visionary' extends our capacity for transformative action in the here and now and for the future. There is a 'visionary' dimension to hoping which needs to be examined in terms of its pragmatics and its consequences.

In Chapter 4, I began to consider the ways in which—as I see it—hope's visionary dimension is connected to processes of concrete change. In this last chapter I want to put that question in the spotlight and ask what can dreaming do to effect change? I will then suggest that attempting to address this question can illuminate some of the more-subtle processes by which change happens, processes that might otherwise be difficult to perceive and appreciate.

I suggest that the starting point for this enquiry is the relationship between hope and attention. In Chapter 1, I described how Nietzsche regarded hope as a torment because the hoper is held in a state of high tension, often as part of a cycle of hope/despair in which expectations are repeatedly quashed. I will now suggest that this conception of 'expectation' is misconstrued. In it, expectation is understood to be distinct from (in no way causally or interactively connected to) what will or will not happen in the future. By contrast, I now want to suggest that making a conceptual distinction between hope and future events prevents us from understanding how hope is, or can be, causal of 'the future' by which I mean that hope can involve a kind of activist function, it can be part of preparing for *and performing* the future. No doubt these last sentences are unclear and, perhaps, have a kind of mystical tone. I realise that further explanation is required.

I am saying that there is no clear dividing line between the present and the future (or indeed, the past). Rather, how these temporal realms come to be demarcated is a matter of social activity and by that logic, 'the future' is always latent in the present because it is made manifest in and through how we render 'the present' meaningful through forms, acts and practices. For example, what I 'am doing' now (in this case, as I type each letter of each of these words) brings me, micro-act-by-micro-act into micro-frames of the 'no longer present', the 'near future', and the 'future'. It does so in the simple example of completing a typed sentence (this sentence, will not be written if I stop typing). And it does so in less trivial cases, such as the digging, with a spoon, of a tunnel, out of a prison and toward a possible 'freedom' … Thus, one can argue, if every single thing we do 'might' be an act capable of change, albeit at times in ways that may be imperceptible, then, as a methodology for effecting change it is absolutely vital to remain vigilant, indeed, hyper-vigilant, to the present. And this is what hope, or effective hoping can do: capacitated, perception heightened by the dream, hope sharpens the senses and can help us to be attentive to the present. This intense focus on our surroundings, on potential opportunities for action, in turn allows for the possibility of change, even if microscopically. Action and imagination are in other words mutually enhancing.

5.2   Moving Mountains?

Sometimes things change quickly, cataclysmically—a meteor hitting the earth for example. Other times things may change at a glacial pace. When things change very slowly that change may be imperceptible. The philosopher and poet Goethe, speaking of mountains and weather once said:

> When we look at mountains, whether from far or near, and see their summits, now glittering in sunshine, now surrounded in mists or wreathed in storm-tossed clouds, now lashed by rain or covered with snow, we attribute all these phenomena to the atmosphere, because all its movements and changes are visible to the eye. To the eye, on the other hand, shapes of the mountains always remain immobile; and because they seem rigid, inactive and at rest, we believe them to be dead. But for a long time I have felt convinced that most manifest atmospheric changes are really due to their imperceptible and secret influence. I believe, that is to say, that, by and large the gravitational force exerted by the earth's mass, especially by its projections, is not constant and equal, but, whether from internal necessity or external accident, it is like a pulse, now increasing, now decreasing. Our means for measuring this oscillation may be too limited and crude, but sensitive reactions of the atmosphere to it are enough to give us sure information about these sensitive forces. When the gravitational pull of the mountains decreases even slightly, this is immediately indicated by the diminished weight and elasticity of the air. The atmosphere can no longer retain the moisture mechanically or chemically diffused through it; the clouds descend, rain falls heavily, and shower clouds move down into the plain. (Goethe date: 31)

Goethe continues to describe what happens when the mountain's gravitational pull increases—the mountains then 'gather' clouds around their summits. Goethe then describes how thunder storms can be understood as 'an inner struggle of electrical forces'. The elasticity of the air, Goethe hypothesizes, is able to absorb more moisture and thus can dissipate clouds. In a signal passage, Goethe then describes how he believed that he had, himself observed, 'the absorption of one such cloud':

> It clung to the steepest summit, tinted by the afterglow of the setting sun. Slowly, slowly, its edges detached themselves, some fleecy bits were drawn off, lifted high up, and then vanished. Little by little, the whole mass disappeared before my eyes, as if it were being spun off from a distaff of an invisible hand. (ibid: 32)

Of course, what Goethe has to say here involves metaphoric attributions ('inner struggle' and so forth). It also involves conjecture and poetic imagination. However, if we are willing to stay with Goethe, it becomes possible to entertain what we conventionally speak of as 'the weather' and its causes, in a more holistic way. Indeed, it is possible to understand Goethe as outlining a methodology—and an epistemology—for knowing about the natural world. This methodology seems to me to be both novel (for the twenty-first century if not for the 18th) and profound in its epistemological consequences.

Goethe speaks of a kind of ecological holisim (nothing is inert, not even the mountains), and, more radically, he speaks of how the 'inert' and invisible can be rendered visible *if* imagination and empirical patience are combined. Making the 'inert' visible (think of a situation in which it seems that, 'nothing is changing') may be possible if we are willing to attend to a phenomenon in Goethe's words (just quoted), 'slowly, slowly' and 'little by little' and this form of attention requires training and endurance. Looking closely, minutely, also involves—often—the use, and at times *improvisatory creation*, of techniques to focus attention. Some of these also involve what we speak of, colloquially, as *prosthetic* technologies (things that extend perception, such as the telescope or microscope) including body technologies (I squint so as to see the horizon more clearly). Others of these involve *proxy* technologies, that is ways of learning about one thing by watching another. (For example, Goethe speaks of the lack of appropriate prosthetic technologies—our, 'means for measuring this oscillation may be too limited and crude'—and he speaks of proxy technologies when he says, 'sensitive reactions of the atmosphere to it are enough to give us sure information about these sensitive forces'—namely that we can learn about the mountains' imperceptible processes by paying close attention to the proxy of the atmosphere.)

The prosthetic and body technologies discussed so far have been physical (I use a telescope or binoculars, I squint so as to see farther, or shield my eyes with my hand so as to block out the sun, I cup my ear with my hand, I open my nostrils so as to smell something more keenly). But they may also involve culture, for example, metaphors, exemplars, aesthetic media such as pictures or literary description, models and—importantly, forms of sensibility. As such, poetic materials recast, as I described in Chapter 4, the present into new forms, thus, as possible futures. So, for example, if I am trying to locate the north star, Polaris, in the night sky, and you tell me that it is located at the end of the 'handle' of the 'little dipper', which in turn I can find by looking straight out from the end of the big dipper, I have a gestalt image, and one of a couple of more readily recognizable objects—a couple of pots or ladles—that I can employ to assist me in locating the object I might otherwise not have found. From then on, locating Polaris may become routine and I can teach others how to find it too.

So too, my attention may also be enhanced through feeling states, emotion or sensibility (we may speak about how we are 'sensitised' to noticing a certain thing). The sensibility of being hopeful is a case in point here: the hope and faith that 'the dream' will eventually 'open itself' is a prime example of this—hope can sensitise us to the present and in ways that enhance our attention to the present so that it becomes hyper-vigilant.

All of these forms of prosthetic and proxy enhancement open up perception. And they open up and enrich the languages we use to talk about causality and change when it occurs through successive, perhaps liminal (in the sense of beyond sensory thresholds) increments, as Goethe's poetic account of the mountains and their gravitational pull did—it enhanced our motivation to attend: poetics gave us, arguably, hope that we would 'see': it quickened our sensibility and made us *want to see* which is half or more than half of the task. While such a statement probably sounds esoteric and mystical put in the way it has so far been put, it can be further clarified.

In Chapter 2, I quoted Les Back who spoke of, 'an attentiveness to the moments when "islands of hope" are established and the social conditions that makes their emergence possible' (2015: n.p.). Back spoke of how, 'an attention to the present and the expectation that something will happen' can, as he put it, 'gift an unforeseen opportunity' (Back 2015: n.p.). I now want to develop this idea—that hope is opportunity-seeking, and that hope involves explicitly pragmatic attention. And that in its attention, hope is, above all, patient.

This patience (hyper-attentiveness to opportunities for realising a dream) is also the quality that makes hope conducive to what Goethe regarded as true empiricism. If love is attentive to the here and now because of the delight that it finds there, and if hate is inattentive because it projects onto its object pre-construed ideas of what is there (without bothering to investigate), hope is arguably hyper-attentive to the here and now because of its fundamental concern with uncovering signs that—as a kind of hypothetical orientation to the future—the things that are hoped for can be justified (and signs of opportunities for making them happen), that is, that the dream will—sometime—be carried. In this regard, then, hope may be regarded as an aesthetic (emotional, sensory) component of knowing, and thus making, the world—phenomena are, in other words, refracted through the prism of hoping.

I am suggesting that hope is a methodological resource for what Goethe termed, 'delicate' or 'gentle empiricism' (*zarte Empirie*). Goethe understood this approach as one in which we 'attend quietly', watching and waiting unobtrusively (Ansdell and Pavlicevic 2010; DeNora 2014) and without attempting to force phenomena into pre-conceptual grids. For Goethe, this 'gentleness' lay at the heart of truly scientific observation (Goethe 2010 [1792]). How, then, is hope a methodological resource both for understanding the world (how can hope contribute to gentle empiricism), *and* for changing the world (how is hope in itself linked to activism)? I suggest the answer to these questions is that dreaming is a way of knowing *and* a way of acting in the world.

5.3   Dreaming as Knowing

No matter how patient we may be, no matter how attentive to detail, there may be things we are not able to observe and yet which are, slowly, happening—Goethe's mountains for example. Conversely, we may be unaware of how we might contribute to effecting change when we think we have done 'nothing'. In other words, hope holds us to a form of attention (looking for signs and opportunities). This attention involves looking for what we might not be able to 'see' and yet which may be undergoing a kind of liminal metamorphosis. How then to open up what may, or may not be, a seemingly imperceptible world of possible changes so that we can see (and conceptualise) that world as containing processes, as in flux and, perhaps, as moving toward a dream (and therefore as allowing us to approach that dream)? Here I think is where we come to the crux of why, at the beginning of this book I suggested that we must not discard the notion that hope involves dreaming and that hoping is most usefully defined as the carrying of a dream.

I have already said, more than once, that hope is highly creative. Hope is creative because it draws together and magnifies resources that carry dreams through bringing, protecting, projecting, infecting. Through these forms of 'carrying' hope uses the imagination of a future as a method of attending to the present. And that imagination creates a liminal space between present and future for the person or people who hope—they are suspended in a virtual state of play (serious play—it may not always consist of 'fun'), inhabiting the dream in the hope that it will—down the line—be carried, realised. It is important now to underline how this dreaming is not—as John Blacking once said of music—an *escape* from reality but an adventure into reality (Blacking 1973: 28): inhabiting the imagination, as we do when we 'carry' in the sense of bringing, protecting, projecting and infecting others/ourselves with things that 'carry' the dream is, simultaneously, virtual and real.

In a study of the dreams of American Civil War (1861–1865) soldiers and their loved ones, the historian Jonathan W. White describes how, before and during and after the American Civil War, it was common practice to record and share one's dreams (and more than thirty years before Freud published his *Interpretation of Dreams* in 1899). When parted, husbands and wives wrote to each other of their dreams, not only dreams of being reunited but dreams of premonition ('we have been so much together of late years that my heart aches when I cannot kiss you goodnight', one wife wrote to her husband and then, in reference to a disturbing dream, 'God grant my dreams may not be warnings'). The idea that dreams were or could be a source of knowledge and prophesy, and the practice of recording and sharing one's dreams was common:

> Many Americans believed that their dreams were windows into the future, and they took their premonitions seriously. At various points during the war, ordinary Americans sent dream reports to their leaders, believing that their night time visions might offer guidance to those in command of the Union and Confederate governments. (White 2017: xv)

I will now suggest that the term, 'prophesy' is not, theoretically, helpful because it conceals more than it reveals. I suggest that the term maintains a boundary between dreams and reality, and between present and future, in ways that pose dreams as premonitions of what 'will happen' and which, as 'premonitions' cannot therefore be explained by rational means. Here I am continuing to develop the point that the present and the future are not distinct, cannot possibly be distinct. I suggest that dreaming is an empirical knowledge-producing activity, as an implicit 'critique' of the present, and as a way of producing knowledge that should not be considered esoteric, and moreover that dreams are actually—and can be seen to be—*causative*—dreams (our visions of how things might be, should be, must be, are becoming) can actually contribute to what 'happens', seemingly 'down the line'. This is a complicated proposition which is perhaps not—at least not yet—helped by repeating that to dream is not to escape from reality but to venture 'into' it. The explanation has something in common with the concept of 'self-fulfilling' prophesy and it has even more in common with the idea that—for the most part tacitly—we routinely enact the categories of reality that we believe are 'given' and fail to see how, in fact, our enactment is bringing them into being and elaborating and strengthening them over time. But it is more complicated yet, since it is attributing to the imagination and the pre-conscious mind a subtle form of intelligence that is a vital resource for making change occur, for realising dreams.

Freud, of course, touched on this theme when he said that dreams offered valid empirical knowledge, describing what he viewed as 'hypermnesic' (the opposite of 'amnesic' or without memory—having exact and vivid memories) dreams:

> That dreams have at their disposal recollections which are inaccessible to the waking state is such a remarkable and theoretically important fact that I should like to draw attention to the point by recording yet other hypermnesic dreams. Maury relates that for some time the word Mussidan used to occur to him during the day. He knew it to be the name of a French city, but that was all. One night he dreamed of a conversation with a certain person, who told him that she came from Mussidan, and, in answer to his question as to where the city was, she replied: "Mussidan is the principal town of a district in the department of Dordogne." On waking, Maury gave no credence to the information received in his dream; but the gazetteer showed it to be perfectly correct. In this case the superior knowledge of the dreamer was confirmed, but it was not possible to trace the forgotten source of this knowledge. (Freud 1899: 21)

Here the content of a dream does not come from a mysterious source but can be explained through the psychology of selective attention. We notice much more, in a given day or split second, than what, cognitively, we are able to register consciously and recall as memory—in part because we may suffer from 'inattentional blindness'—in other words, our attention is captured or structured in relation to what we are cued to notice and what seems to be relevant to our preconceptions of what 'is there' to be seen (DeNora 2014: 6–7; Simons and Chabris 1999). When dream during sleep, however, what we 'had not noticed earlier' can resurface, albeit in combinations and formats that may be at variance from the original context, recombining, repositioning, introducing novel features. And as with dreams during sleep, so too, with dreams during waking: a dream allows us to 'open up' our senses, to be hyper-attentive, and there-fore' hypermnesic' to features of our environments and social relations that, against the foil of the dream, may be more brightly illuminated. The dream provides, in other words, a future-oriented lens with which to view the present and as such it is a prosthetic technology for 'seeing' what otherwise might be invisible. Dreams, in other words, can enhance our perception and, in relation to being able to carry those dreams, they make us more resourceful. The process is circular.

The production of dreams as a form of activism is, of course, part of what art and artists do. The surrealists made a feature of this resource and one of the best treatments of the social and epistemological func-tion of art as dreaming can be found in Robert Witkin's (1995), *Art and Social Structure*. In a section near the end of that work, Witkin considers surrealism and makes a case for dreaming as an activity that can, 'infuse reality with a profoundly transformed and enriched imagination' (1995: 199). He suggests that dreams offer a means for transformation because, 'as Freud had pointed out, [they] knew none of the ordinary distinctions which kept here from there, now from then and this from that' (1995: 199). As Witkin puts it:

> The dream was the reality that went unacknowledged in the modern world of rational institutions…[it] is the ultimate machinery of world-making. What is made in the dream is not the world as such but the structured sensibility that is to be the instrument—that is, the machinery—of world-making. (1995: 200–201)

It is the 'structured sensibility' of hoping, that, as I have argued, offers, in Witkin's words, a 'machinery' of world-making. Hope's sensibility is, in other words, activist. Dreaming and acting are connected and this is why the dream is integral to the activity of hope and its orientation to change.

Throughout this short book I have understood hope's form of dreaming in a broad and inclusive way as something that is oriented to what is not present but which could be present in future times. A dream includes day dreams, longing, memories, visions of situations, relations, circumstances, conditions. It involves using the imagination, fantasising, and creative practices of rendering dreams as fiction, image, poetry, conversational topics, music. We make dreams known to ourselves and others by focusing on objects which we protect and project and we catch dreams as they are carried, infectiously, by others and by ourselves (we can re-infect ourselves through our projection activities). Unlike dreams we have at night, these dreams are part of our waking hours, though of course they may also be part of what we dream of when we sleep. They need not be prolonged, as in 'day dreams' to count as dreams either—there are micro-moments of attention where we have fleeting 'alternate visions' of things, as in when we mishear or 'see' things that are not 'there' or as in when we have 'flashes' of 'insight' which pass in an instant and may be forgotten, or when activities and people come together in lightening moments of collective effervescence as 'optimal moments' in Pavlicevic's view (Pavlicevic 2010). We need, in other words, empirically, to expand our conception of what it can mean to 'dream'. And we need to study, as I have described in Chapter 4, the processes by which we acquire dreams—through, for example, our engagement with (our intro-jection of) cultural, aesthetic materials which help us to recognise and flesh out what we dream of, to put dreams into words, images, and songs.

5.4 Dreaming as Pragmatic Acting

If dreaming is epistemologically productive and, once again, *creative*, then dreaming is a resource for action. It assists us to locate the—as it were—possible 'chinks in the armour' of 'what is given'. It sharpens our wits, in other words because dreaming, understood as *envisioning*, can train observation and promote innovation. Dreaming opens the imag-ination in ways that may recalibrate attention can create new ways of imaging the past, present, and future, incrementally, and often in ways that we may not recognise with conscious thought.

Think of someone who is trying to achieve something that is seem-ingly impossible—to escape from prisoner of war camp, to ascend the Matterhorn, to make water flow uphill, to learn to play the violin or to play a wind instrument without seemingly taking a breath, to pull a rabbit from a hat. All of these things may, initially, seem impossible (in relation to making water flow uphill, Chandra Mukerji has spoken of this process as 'impossible engineering' [Mukerji 2009]), and yet each of these examples has proved has to be not impossible—to be possible and doable. Yet each would have been impossible if it had not initially been dreamed of and in ways that drew the dream in contact with being on the lookout for signs and opportunities—and techniques—for its realisation.

Think, for example of how the dream of escape can fuel the motivation for escape of prisoners of war in ways that both given physical energy and also fire the imagination and can lead to ingenious techniques for avoiding detection, and for producing what has to be done (improvised tools for digging, for supporting the back while digging, for maintaining the psychic strength to carry on). Think of how playing the saxophone for five or ten minutes without breathing involves a painstaking and time-consuming practice of learning how to take micro-breathes through the nose while pushing air out to the instrument from puffed cheeks such that, to the naked ear and eye, you 'are not taking any breaths'.

These achievements require considerable attention to detail, a kind of patient watching, waiting, and noticing opportunities, that might afford (even micro-incremental) advance. Through this work, slowly, slowly, change occurs, but the moment at which it happens may never be known. Imaginative action does not, in other words, simply keep us poised or ready to jump when 'the moment arrives'. To the contrary, it is active—it is constantly and resourcefully looking for ways *incrementally*, as in building a pathway (Ansdell and DeNora 2016) to bring the present into closer alignment with the future. Consider the image of the shaman and the rope, as discussed by Averill et al.Chon (1990) (who are in turn discussing Desroche's 1979 sociological study of hope):

> Desroche (1979) introduced his sociological study of hope by reference to a metaphor...Hope is a rope...attributed to the 17th century German mystic Angelus Silesius. As Desroche points out in many mystical traditions the fakir or shaman throws a rope in the air (or alternatively the rope may fall from the sky). Although the rope appears to be attached to nothing substantial, it nevertheless holds fast, allowing the fakir to ascend.

Desroche believes this metaphor reflects something basic about human nature namely, the 'constitutive imagination'. Human beings, held down by the weight of necessities, find something like a rope by which they can ascend to a higher plane. 'To the observer, it seems that there is nothing to keep it [the rope] up, except for the impalpable and inconsistent worlds of fantasy, wanderings and absurdity' (p. 3). Like the rope of the fakir, hope also defies the gravity of the everyday world, and allows the individual to ascend to a higher plane of reality. (1980: n.p.)

Averill et al. seem to imply that the only form of constraint ('gravity') defied by hope is imaginative and that hope's ascendancy, its defiance of gravity, is confined to *mental* rearrangement—metaphorically ascending to a 'higher plane of reality'. Here, the person who hopes, like the mystic, turns away from worldly matters and enters the life of the mind, spiritual contemplation, retreat. This perspective is mentalist, idealist and mystical and it is not the perspective I am seeking to advance on dreaming and change. By contrast, as I have been discussing in the examples of escape, tightrope walking, mountain climbing, breathless saxophone playing, conjuring, and so forth, I am suggesting that hope is in fact a form of dream-fueled, everyday empiricism that in turn fosters a kind of engineering mentality that is ultimately pragmatic. It *is* entirely possible, in other words, to climb something with no visible means of support—*but* that activity involves resourceful marshalling of many micro-resources that make the activity of climbing possible.

Indeed, in the 'real world' this is what world-class rock climbers do on a regular basis, locating hand and foot holds that, to non-climbers, are invisible. These holds are invisible because what counts as a 'hold' only emerges in relation to the advanced technique of inserting fingers into folds or cracks, exploiting minute grooves or dimples in a rock face, and careful, strategic balance. As Antoine Hennion has said, these 'movements' involve indistinct mergers of rock and body:

What climbing shows is not that the geological rock is a social construction, but that it is a reservoir of differences that can be brought into being. The climber makes the rock as the rock makes the climber. The differences are indeed in the rock, and not in the 'gaze' that is brought to it. But these are not brought to bear without the activity of the climb which makes them present. (Hennion 2007: 100–101)

Part of the problem of not seeing what affords the activity of, in this case, improbable climbing, is lack of motivation, inspiration, indeed, the very things of which, we might say, serious dream carrying ('making present' the dream) is made. Hope, then, is both the thing that gives the hoper strength and patience and ingenuity (to continue to find the folds in the rock, for example), and through what it gives, hope is a method for achieving its aim. Once again—hoping needs to dream.

If we think about activities of hoping as offering us case studies in the history of the present moment we can begin to entertain different, and perhaps more poetically enhanced understandings of how we move from past to present to future (and from future back to present and past—as when we remember or adjust our aspirations or dreams in light of where we have gone or where we think we have gone or are going) and what it is about this time traveling that contributes to effecting change, if not necessarily in 'rational' or 'goal-oriented' ways. And not necessarily ever a topic of conscious reflection. Gro Tronadalen who has written about the present moment in music therapy picks up on this point when she says simply but with great wisdom, that, 'important moments are often unspoken and relational, and they happen in a moment' (2016: 17). Trondalen describes how sometimes, in a matter of seconds, things— vitality forms, relational realities between people—change and that a micro-lens calibrated for perceiving micro-events can show us just how change occurs (that is how the present becomes the future, how some things mutate or morph to take on new aspects, leaving behind old aspects) and in ways that—when examined from further away, through a wider lens—might become invisible. Looking at change microscopi- cally dissolves the boundaries between past, present, and future, indeed it draws these time frames together, and I have written about this issue in relation to change before:

... the interconnections between ... three time frames of [an] event [that draw] past into present and future. ... This triple time is ...what we do together ... in relation to each other and our environment ... [It] reconstructs us and repositions us for future action and identities. How this process actually transpires is a question for ethnography, for discussion between participants, and self-reflection: 'We are different now, but how did this change occur?' we ask one another. (DeNora 2013: 143)

A focus on hoping as a series of present moments calls attention to how, if we find ways of looking (and listening) closely – microscopically in other words—we can begin to 'see' what otherwise was invisible, namely little-by-little adjustments that, potentially, can bring into effect long-lasting and often-large forms of change. And it calls attention to technique, to how people locate resources for those adjustments—chalk for the hands of a climber, metaphors about how one is growing from a 'little shoot', new ways of seeing/noticing that allow for the perception of resources and loopholes and chinks in the armor of the 'status quo'. And—fold upon fold, little by little—it is possible to end up at the summit. There is, therefore, always reason for hope, understood as the carrying of a dream. By that logic, who is there that cannot climb a mountain?

5.5   Who Cannot Hope?

In his poignant poem, *The Old Fools* Philip Larkin's wonders about what it is like not to be able to remember any more (the final line of the poem is, 'We shall find out'). As he muses, he suggests that:

Perhaps being old is having lighted rooms
    Inside your head, and people in them, acting.
    People you know, yet can't quite name, each looms
    Like a deep loss restored... (Larkin 1974: 13–14)

Of course, all of us (or most of us), old and young, have 'lighted rooms' inside our heads. By that logic, why not also people suffering from memory impairment, dementia, Alzheimer's disease, brain trauma or other cognitive/neuro issues. These things increasingly touch most families and have touched mine (DeNora 2017). Many of us will be familiar with how people suffering from dementia may regularly pack a bag and go for a wander, or in their own meaning system, speak of 'setting out for home', even when they are in fact living 'at home'.

We might on first consideration think this strange. On reflection, perhaps it highlights how the hopeful impulse never leaves us, how we continue to seek, even when we may become confused about what it is we are seeking as we carry a kind of dream. And yet, one might suggest that the differences between the person 'with' and 'without' mental capacity are not, in context of hoping, so very different. For even so-called 'more sentient' people may hope in imprecise, perhaps 'confused' ways, may 'wander' mentally (and sometimes physically, but have the presence of mind to label it, 'a hike' or 'an amble'). We all at times have hoped for half-articulated, ambiguous things and we may have hoped without necessarily putting our hopes into explicit words, let alone goals we identify as ones we wish to attain. For example, how many of us have found ourselves 'wandering' in a shop, 'in search' of something but not sure what it is (and this is often in response to a cluster of pushes and pulls from marketeers and our own everyday aspirations, as described by Brownlie [2014]). So too, when in pain (say you injure a knee badly and are lying in bed) you may not every moment explicitly be thinking of 'what you hope for' ('I want this knee to get better'). But as you lie there, applying ice, compression, elevation, you might suddenly think of an image, a snippet of conversation, a past 'nice' moment, a bit of music and it might not only please you or sooth you but remind you—in a fleeting and not necessarily conscious way—of where you 'hope' to be in a few weeks' time. If asked later, you might not even be aware that, in that moment, you had a 'lighted room' in your head.

And so too, in examples that perhaps fewer of us may know about first-hand—the situation of being in what is often termed a 'vegetative state'. Is it possible, then, for that person themselves to hope? Music therapist Wolfgang Schmid describes his work with a 44-year-old man ('Marc'). Schmid describes how, initially, he tried to create a 'familiar atmosphere' by performing for Marc music that, prior to his accident, Marc had loved (Pink Floyd; Dire Straits). Schmid noted that Marc's embodied patterns of response did not alter—he remained in a high state of arousal, breathing heavily, restless. Schmid describes how he:

> felt very strongly that I was not able to reach him by making music for him. is led me to the idea of finally improvising on a kantele, a little string instrument, without addressing him or awaiting any reaction, but closing our first session with music. Later on I could see on the video, that Marc's heavy breathing led to minimal, involuntarily movement of his head to the left hand side. (Schmid 2017: 189)

In Schmid's second encounter with Marc, Schmid describes how Marc's arousal levels were, once again, high. Schmid decided to offer improvisational music therapy, taking Marc's breathing movements as his starting point for the joint music-making. Schmid responded to the tempo of Marc's breathing and added some chords to—cautiously— mix music with movement. Schmid then began to sing in what he describes as a deliberate attempt to match Marc's expressive movements, 'allowing for the experience of sensory integration' (190). When, later on, Marc suddenly stopped all movement, Schmid did the same, allowing the silence to function as a musical pause, and thus creating between them a sense of musical collaboration. Schmid describes how when he resumed playing he deliberately altered the music, now employing waltz tempo and rhythm (ONE-two-three). After a few minutes, Marc again stopped all movement and opened his eyes and looked directly at Schmid. Schmid took that as his cue to pause again, allowing Marc to have control over how and when they ended that music session. As Schmid puts it, the music was created *with* Marc, not *for* him.

Schmid speaks of the, 'bodily-emotional situatedness of the man and the music therapist' and how that situatedness produces an, 'area of exchange for a non-verbal, affect-driven communication' (Schmid 2017: 186). '[P]laying with the affect', Schmid writes, 'is the main topic for the encounter, promoting self-organizational processes in both individuals involved'.

The term, 'playing with affect' highlights what Schmid then describes as 'affect attunement' (a term from Stern 2010 [1985]) and developed within music therapy by Pavlicevic (2002) through the notion of 'dynamic forms', or musical forms that reproduce feeling properties (Schmid 2017: 189). Through the medium of music, 'Marc' could be returned to the intra-affective world and in ways that transformed his embodied state from highly tense to more relaxed, to seemingly incapable of voluntary movement, to control. As Schmid observes:

> Marc presented levels of activity, intentionality and interest in interpersonal contact in the improvised encounter that had not been observed outside music therapy. In music therapy, he could partly regain his interactive potential, and share his state of being within a communicative ecology, relieving his isolation for a period of time. (Schmid 2017: 191)

One must take great care when speculating or imputing motives to others, indeed, even to ourselves. Might it also then have been possible that Marc now had at least one thing to anticipate– namely, further opportunities to engage in mutual affect regulation through mutual music making and thus, perhaps, also something for which to hope (finding a way of being in which there are still creative outlets, connections to others and, perhaps, even if 'impossible' the possibility of recovery)? And might this have been—given the presence of a highly skilled music therapist who was 'listening' or attending closely and 'gently' and building upon what Marc could do (his resources such as patterns of breathing)—a realistic thing to 'hope' for? In this respect, Schmid's study and the quality of his interactions with Marc highlight the importance of improvisation (recall that the first time Schmid met with Marc he attempted to use pre-composed musical material—Pink Floyd; Dire Straits—which failed to 'reach' Marc, in the sense that Marc did not exhibit any alteration in his high level of tension or in offering signs of recognition of others). By contrast, turning to improvised format, allowed Marc to contribute, to help to shape the musical event, to gain a kind of musical validation or amplification of his signs of 'being there' and to be part of an expressive, creative ecology in which he could participate and help to furnish or co-create. Increasingly, the value of improvisation is being recognised more generally by scholars in music education and music psychology where creativity is conceptualised as a distributed property of groups, where the concept of 'choice' is greatly enriched, where the lofty requirement of 'shared understanding' within improvised musical situations is deconstructed and discarded in favour of the participants' 'investment in the process' (MacDonald and Wilson 2020: 168), and where that investment in the process, the ability to participate and the recognition of being a participant, and the empowerment that flows from these things, is explicitly understood as a condition, and indeed cause, of wellbeing. And this brings us back to what it is hope does, and who can hope.

The case study from Schmid highlights the importance of micro-moments of relief, alleviation, palliation and space in which to be expressive These moments allow for, at the least, glimpses of a better, desired, future situation. Of course, it is possible, sometimes probable, that these glimpses will not add up to 'getting better', or even to a substantial improvement in 'quality of life'. And indeed, in Marc's case, Schmid writes that, after he and Marc had met for nine sessions of music therapy, 'Marc' contracted pneumonia and died. Were Marc's hopes unrealised? Or, in fact, was his (hypothetical) hope of making contact with the world again realised in these musical encounters (and perhaps elsewhere and perhaps in ways that interrelated)? I cannot possibly presume to answer such a question, indeed, perhaps not even the person in question can answer such a question. But I can suggest that we our thinking about hope should embrace how hope can be lodged in both long-term and short-term arcs. So, it may be less important to ask if the effects of the music therapy 'accumulated' in way that led to longer-term change for Marc, enabling him, if not to 'get better', at least to experience growing improvement, if not physical, then social and in terms of quality of life than to ask about micro-moments of 'better times' for Marc, ones in which he could be lodged within realistic frameworks and networks of hoping (whatever he might hope for surely would include moments of musically produced meetings and perhaps therefore respite and surely whatever anyone might hope on his behalf would as well?). The palliative care specialist (and music therapist) Nigel Hartley makes this point eloquently in his consideration of an individual music therapy session with a client who, in a moment of musical interaction, seemed to find meaning, release, or something. When asked, did it make a difference to the quality of her life, Hartley said:

> I think in asking this we are in danger of losing the sense of the *now* and what's really important – the health system we work in always wants to ask: Did it make a difference? It certainly made a difference at that moment. (Hartley 2009: 66)

What I take from this thought, in relation to hope and hoping is that we need to be highly attentive to the micro-moments within which hope may flourish (even if it then recedes and does not return or grow). We ned to focus on these micro-moments just as much as we might otherwise concern ourselves with so-called 'large'-scale waves of hope that can gather and push individuals and groups forward like a force, as in social movements and activist endeavours: the time of the rose, in other words, is to paraphrase T. S. Elliot, no smaller than the time of the yew tree (cf Elliot's Four Quartets [Little Gidding]). In relation to music therapy, sometimes minute details can be enormously important in helping to kindle micro-moments of hoping:

> *Auld Lang Syne*– the final goodbye sequence today. This continues this physical and musical phenomenology of connecting and associating people in/through music. The song literally gathers together almost everyone in the room– and these people are both present and aware of themselves in music, but also of each other. (which I suppose is the point of the song!)
> Gunter's volcano voice wells and climaxes, Sarah looks towards him in admiration. Visible too are many of the small forms [of] participation …: nods, tiny movements of people giving something musically to the collective effervescence. More is happening here than 'should happen' under the circumstances–this is what hope is about. (Ansdell, Reflections on Care for Music)

In all three of these cases the person who packs a bag with a mixture of photographs, toiletries, potatoes, and old greeting cards and goes for a wander in hope of finding 'home', the person who 'wanders' mentally while hoping to get over a bout of pain or discomfort, and the person who, with only minute and scarce resources available for self-expression and for feeling, is enabled to take part in music making, hope is not a matter of rational cognitive planning so much as an impulse and a desire for change—of any sort, for any length of time, and of any quantity—and it is a way of acting. These forms of hopefulness, hoping and realized hopes are in turn connected to fleeting and fragmented visions (and feeling impulses) of whatever it is we might be dreaming about, what, ultimately, we hope to achieve or find (to our dream-quests as it were) and in ways that underline the capacity to orient to a future in ways that do not require propositional knowledge or verbal skill. All of us can hope, hope is good for all of us. The question that remains therefore is under what circumstances are opportunities for hope—felt or verbally expressed—produced, facilitated, and constrained.

Not everyone will be in a situation where they are able to marshal the resources (cultural materials, interpersonal support, time, space, confidence and a sense of believing in what might—just—be possible). It is entirely possible to tamp down hope and to suppress the kinds of things that otherwise nurture hope and what can be hoped for. There is, in short, a social distribution of opportunities for hoping and for who may hope for what and that distribution is a topic for critical sociology. It is also a matter of human rights.

5.6   Social Hope

Hope, then, is a form of action. It is not by any means the same as wanting or desiring things, or setting a goal and a plan for achieving something. Hope is complicated. It is poetic. To speak of one's hope is not to speak of what one might like to 'receive'—a wish-list of birthday presents or a 'letter to Santa' or a prayer asking one's god to 'give' one things in return for x, y or z. Hope is more noble, more emotional, far less calculating, often less clear or targeted, much closer emotionally to longing, and love. For this reason, learning how to hope, what to hope for, and when to hope (and when to do something other than hope) is part of human emotional intelligence and part of our capacity for resilience throughout the life course. So, learning how to help each other to hope together—and act hopefully together—is arguably a core human social project and—I would argue—critical to a society's public health. Hartley and Ridley (2016: n.p.) describes how activities such as music therapy can 'pull' people out of isolation' and thereby prevent social death, because, 'even in the depths of despair and destruction, there is the potential for beauty, for truth and for love'. Being hopeful is, I suggest, both a resource for and a product of this kind of love, and the potential social immortality that it fosters. Being hopeful, actively carrying a dream in all the senses here described, is ultimately a way of remaining attached (not becoming dislodged from) to the 'mountain' of human solidarity.

The thesis of this book has been that hope, as a way of holding and carrying dreams keeps us focused and strong. As we make hope, individually, collectively, in and through the many ways we play creatively with time, we produce a warp for future realities. Hope is never passive: it is a technique of world-making—we project our hopes into the world and in ways that alter those worlds and the ways they are perceived. This imaginative activity involves showcasing to ourselves and others thoughts and images of 'the future' and images of 'the past' (including of course ourselves within these). It involves sidelining other thoughts and images that might lead us to despair. To hope is to be creative and, even when conducted in isolation, hope is social in origins, in orientation and in its potential consequences, rearranging horizons of experience and expectation. Hope foregrounds and backgrounds features of our lives. It knits the now to the then and the later and does so according to the patterns we improvise and negotiate with others, and imagined others, in the world. It embellishes stories of what will or can happen. And this activity not only makes it easier to endure the now; it is also generative of what we can do from within, and about, the now as it becomes the then. In this sense, hope is the ultimate dream we carry—when we hope we are imbued with purpose and meaning, and we are connected to a vision of the world. And as such, we are emboldened and empowered to carry very many more particular dreams together and individually—in all the senses of carrying we have considered—thereby making what is dreamed of as the future present.

References

Ansdell, G., & DeNora, T. (2016). *Musical Pathways in Recovery: Community Music Therapy and Mental Wellbeing*. London: Routledge.

Ansdell, G., & Pavlicevic, M. (2010). Practicing "Gentle Empiricism": The Nordoff Robbins Research Heritage. *Music Therapy Perspectives, 28*(2), 131–139.

Averill, J., Caitlin, G., & Chon, K. K. (1990). *The Rules of Hope*. New York: Springer Verlag.

Back, L. (2015). Blind Pessimism and the Sociology of Hope. *Discovering Sociology*, Issue 27. Retrieved on April 12 from https://discoversociety.org/2015/12/01/blind-pessimism-and-the-sociology-of-hope/.

Blacking, J. (1973). *How Musical Is Man*. Seattle: University of Washington Press.

Brownlie, J. (2014). *Ordinary Relationships: A Sociological Study of Emotions, Reflexivity and Culture*. Basingstoke: Palgrave MacMillan.

DeNora, T. (2014). *Making Sense of Reality: Culture and Perception in Everyday Life*. London: Sage.

DeNora, T. (2015 [2013]). *Music Asylums: Wellbeing Through Music in Everyday Life*. London: Routledge.

DeNora, T. (2017). My Bonnie Dearie. In T. Stickley & S. Clift (Eds.), *Arts, Health, and Wellbeing: A Theoretical Inquiry for Practice* (pp. 85–106). Cambridge: Cambridge Scholars Press.

Desroche, H. (1979). *The Sociology of Hope*. London: Routledge, Keagen & Paul.

Freud, S. (1997 [1899]). *The Interpretation of Dreams* (A. A. Brill, Trans.). Ware, Hertfordshire: Wordsworth Classics.

Hartley, N. (2009). *The Creative Arts in Palliative Care: The Art of Dying. Consent and Deceit in Pain Medicine*. The British Pain Society. Retrieved on April 22, 2020 from https://www.britishpainsociety.org/static/uploads/resources/files/2009_transcript__FINAL.pdf.

Hartley, N., & Ridley, A. (2016). Creativity, Discipline and the Arts at the End of Life: An Interview with Nigel Hartley. Approaches: An Interdisciplinary [Special Issue]. *Journal of Music Therapy, 8*(1), 81–84. Retrieved on June 27, 2020 from http://approaches.gr/wp-content/uploads/2016/05/8-Approaches_812016_hartley-i20151129.pdf.

Hennion, A. (2007). These Things That Hold Us Together. *Cultural Sociology, 1*(1), 97–114.

Larkin, P. (1974). *High Windows*. London: Faber & Faber.

MacDonald, R., & Wilson, G. (2020). *The Art of Becoming: How Group Improvisation Works*. Oxford: Oxford University Press.

Mukerji, C. (2009). *Impossible Engineering: Technology and Territoriality in the Canal du Midi*. Princeton: Princeton University Press.

Pavlicevic, M. (2002). Dynamic Interplay in Clinical Improvisation. *Voices: A World Forum for Music Therapy, 2*(2).

Pavlicevic, M. (2010). Reflection: Let the Music Work: Optimal Moments of Collaborative Musicing. In B. Stige, G. Ansdell, C. Elefant, & M. Pavlicevic (Eds.), *Where Music Helps*. Farnham: Ashgate.

Schmid, W. (2017). Being Together—Exploring the Modulation of Affect in Improvisational Music Therapy with a Man in a Persistent Vegetative State—A Qualitative Single Case Study. *Health Psychology Report, 2*(5), 186 192. Retrieved on July 10, 2020 from https://www.termedia.pl/Being-together-Exploring-the-modulation-of-affect-in-improvisational-music-the rapy-with-a-man-in-a-persistent-vegetative-state-a-qualitative-single-case-stu dy,74,28789,1,1.html.

Simons, D. J., & Chabris, C. (1999). Gorillas in Our Midst: Sustained Inattentional Blindness for Dynamic Events. *Perception, 28*(9), 1059–1074.

Stern, D. N. (2010). *Forms of Vitality: Exploring Dynamic Experience in Psychology and the Arts*. Oxford: Oxford University Press.

Trondalen, G. (2016). *Relational Music Therapy: An Intersubjective Perspective*. Dallas, TX: Barcelona Publishers.

von Goethe, J. W. (2010 [1792]). Experiment as a Mediator of Subject and Object. *In Context #24* (Fall), 19–23.

White, J. W. (2017). *Midnight in American: Darkness, Sleep and Dreaming During the Civil War*. Chapell Hill: University of North Carolina Press.

Witkin, R. W. (1995). *Art and Social Structure*. Cambridge: Polity Press.

References

Alaszewski, A., & Wilkinson, I. (2014). The Paradox of Hope for Working Age Adults Recovering from Stroke. *Health, 19*(2), 172–187.

Aldridge, D. (2004). *Health, the Individual and Integrated Medicine: Revisiting an Aesthetic of Health Care.* London: Jessica Kingsley Publishers.

Alessi, M. G., & Bennett, J. M. (2020). Mental Health Is the Health of the Whole Body: How Psychoneuroimmunology Can Inform & Improve Treatment. *Journal of Evaluation in Clinical Practice, 26*(5), 1539–1547.

Ansdell, G. (2014). *How Music Helps: In Music Therapy and Everyday Life.* London: Routledge.

Ansdell, G., & DeNora, T. (2016). *Musical Pathways in Recovery: Community Music Therapy and Mental Wellbeing.* London: Routledge.

Ansdell, G., & Pavlicevic, M. (2010). Practicing "Gentle Empiricism": The Nordoff Robbins Research Heritage. *Music Therapy Perspectives, 28*(2), 131–139.

Antonovsky, A. (1987). *Unraveling the Mystery of Health: How People Manage Stress and Stay Well.* San Francisco, CA: Jossey-Bass Publishers.

Appadurai, A. (2013). *The Future as Cultural Fact: Essays on the Global Condition.* London: Verso.

Atkinson, P. (2020). *Writing Ethnographically.* London: Sage.

Auden, W. H. (1940). *Another Time.* London: Random House.

Averill, J., Caitlin, G., & Chon, K. K. (1990). *The Rules of Hope*. New York: Springer Verlag.

Awed, S. H. (2017). 'We Are Not Free, Admit It...But We Cling Onto Tomorrow': Imagination as a Tool for Coping in Disempowering Situations. In B. Wagoner, I. Bresco de Luna, & S. Awad (Eds.), *The Psychology of Imagination: History, Theory and New Research Horizons* (pp. 267–281). Charlotte, NC: Information Age Publishing Inc.

Back, L. (2015). Blind Pessimism and the Sociology of Hope. *Discovering Sociology*, Issue 27. Retrieved on April 12 from https://discoversociety.org/2015/12/01/blind-pessimism-and-the-sociology-of-hope/.

Bar, R. E., & Gibson, E. (2013). *Building a Culture of Hope: Enriching Schools with Optimism and Opportunity*. Bloomington, IN: Solution Tree Press.

Batt-Rawden, K. B. (2007). Music as a Transfer of Faith: Towards Recovery and Healing. *Journal of Research in Nursing, 12*(1), 87–99.

Berlant, L. (2011). *Cruel Optimism*. Durham, NC: Duke University Press.

Blacking, J. (1973). *How Musical Is Man*. Seattle: University of Washington Press.

Bloch, E. (1986). *The Principle of Hope* (Vols. 1–3). Cambridge, MA: The MIT Press.

Bloch, E. (2000). *The Spirit of Utopia*. Palo Alto: Stanford University Press.

Bloeser, C., & Stahl, T. (2017). Hope. In E. N. Zalta (Ed.), *The Stanford Encyclopedia of Philosophy* (Spring 2017 ed.). Retrieved on June 20, 2020 from https://plato.stanford.edu/archives/spr2017/entries/hope/.

Bonde, L. O., Ruud, E., Strand Skånland, M., & Trondalen, G. (Eds.). (2013). *Musical Life Stories: Narratives on Health Musicking*. Oslo: Norges Musikkhøgskole Publikasjoner.

Brown, J. (2003). *Ernst Bloch and the Utopian Imagination*. Eras. Retrieved on May 30, 2020 from https://www.monash.edu/arts/philosophical-historical-international-studies/eras/past-editions/edition-five-2003-november/ernst-bloch-and-the-utopian-imagination#notes1.

Brown, N. (2015). Metrics of Hope: Disciplining Affect in Oncology. *Health, 2*(19), 119–136.

Brownlie, J. (2014). *Ordinary Relationships: A Sociological Study of Emotions, Reflexivity and Culture*. Basingstoke: Palgrave MacMillan.

Buck-Morss, S. (2002). *Dreamworld and Catastrophe: The Passing of Mass Utopia in East and West*. Cambridge, MA: MIT.

Calvin, J. (2008). *Institutes of the Christian Religion* (H. Beveredge, Trans.). Peabody, MA: Hendrickson's Publishers.

Caroll, A. E. (2014, October 6). The Placebo Effect Doesn't Apply Just to Pills. *New York Times*. Retrieved on March 29, 2020 from https://www.nytimes.com/2014/10/07/upshot/the-placebo-effect-doesnt-apply-just-to-pills.html.

Casey, E. (2000). *Remembering: A Phenomenological Study* (2nd ed.). Bloomington and Indianapolis, IN: Indiana University Press.

Chödrön, P. (2007). *When Things Fall Apart: Heart Advice for Difficult Times*. London: Harper Collins.

Claeys, G. (2017). *Dysutopia: A Natural History*. Oxford: Oxford University Press.

Claeys, G. (2020). *Utopia: The History of an Idea*. London: Thames and Hudson.

Coles, R., & Roma, T. (2008). *House Calls with William Carlos Williams, MD*. New York: Power House Books.

Coward, R. (1985). *Female Desire: Women's Sexuality Today*. London: Paladin.

Crawford, P. P., Brown, B., Baker, C., Tischler, V., & Abrams, B. (2015). *Health Humanities*. Basingstoke: Palgrave Macmillan.

Crawford, P., Brown, B., & Charise, A. (2020). *The Routledge Companion to Health Humanities*. London: Routledge.

Daykin, N. (2020). *Arts, Health and Wellbeing: A Critical Perspective on Research, Policy and Practice*. London: Routledge.

Daykin, N., McClean, S., & Bunt, L. (2007). Creativity, Identity and Healing: Participants' Accounts of Music Therapy in Cancer Care. *Health, 1*(3), 349–370.

Deneraz, K. (2019). *Opinion: 'I Hope to See My Mother Again': Stolen Childhoods of Yazidi Children Returning from ISIS Captivity*. Thomas Reuters Foundation News. Retrieved on March 24, 2020 from https://news.trust.org/item/20190803071323-b7d5v/.

DeNora, T. (1995). *Beethoven and the Construction of Genius: Aesthetic Politics in Vienna 1790–1803*. Berkeley, Los Angeles and London: Unveristy of California Press.

DeNora, T. (2000). *Music in Everyday Life*. Cambridge: Cambridge University Press.

DeNora, T. (2003). *After Adorno: Rethinking Music Sociology*. Cambridge: Cambridge University Press.

DeNora, T. (2012). Resounding the Great Divide: Theorising Music in Everyday Life at the end of Life. *Mortality, 17*(2), 92–105.

DeNora, T. (2014). *Making Sense of Reality: Culture and Perception in Everyday Life*. London: Sage.

DeNora, T. (2015 [2013]). *Music Asylums: Wellbeing Through Music in Everyday Life*. London: Routledge.

DeNora, T. (2017). My Bonnie Dearie. In T. Stickley & S. Clift (Eds.), *Arts, Health, and Wellbeing: A Theoretical Inquiry for Practice* (pp. 85–106). Cambridge: Cambridge Scholars Press.

Desroche, H. (1979). *The Sociology of Hope*. London: Routledge, Keagen & Paul.

Dickinson, E. (1997). *Everyman's Poetry: Emily Dickinson*. London: Dent.

Eagleton, T. (2015). *Hope Without Optimism*. Charlottesville: University of Virginia Press.

Ehrenreich, B. (2009). *Bright Sided: How the Relentless Promotion of Positive Thinking Has Undermined America*. New York: Metropolitan Books.

Ekeland, T.-J. (1997). The Healing Context and Efficacy in Psychotherapy: Psychotherapy and the Placebo Phenomenon. *International Journal of Psychotherapy, 2*(1), 77–87.

Eliot, T. S. (2001). *The Four Quartets*. London: Faber.

Eyerman, R. (2019). *Memory, Trauma and Identity*. Basingstoke: Palgrave Macmillan.

Eyerman, R., & Jameson, A. (1998). *Music and Social Movements*. Cambridge: Cambridge University Press.

Fancourt, D. (2014). An Introduction to the Psychoneuroimmunology of Music: History, Future Collaboration and a Research Agenda. *Psychology of Music, 44*(2), 168–182.

Fancourt, D., & Finn, S. (2019). *What Is the Evidence on the Role of the Arts in Improving Health and Well-being?* Copenhagen: World Health Organisation.

Festinger, L. (2009 [1956]). *When Prophesy Fails*. London: Pinter and Martin.

Fine, G. A. (2012). *Tiny Publics: A Theory of Group Action and Culture*. New York: Russel Sage Foundation.

Finness, D. G., Kaptchuk, T. J., Miller, F., & Benedetti, F. (2010). Biological, Clinical and Ethical Advances of Placebo Effects. *The Lancet, 375*(9715), 686–695.

Foer, F. (2019, September 20). Greta Thunberg Is Right to Panic. *The Atlantic Monthly*. Retrieved on March 21, 2020 from https://www.theatlantic.com/ideas/archive/2019/09/greta-thunbergs-despair-is-entirely-warranted/598492/.

Foucault, M. (1991). Governmentality (R. Braidotti, Trans., and revised by C. Gordon, in G. Burchell, C. Gordon, & P. Miller [Eds.]), *The Foucault Effect: Studies in Governmentality* (pp. 87–104). Chicago, IL: University of Chicago Press.

Frankl, V. E. (2004 [1946]). *Man's Search for Meaning*. London: Ebury.

Freud S. (1997 [1899]). *The Interpretation of Dreams* (A. A. Brill, Trans.). Ware, Hertfordshire: Wordsworth Classics.

Gibbs, A. (2001). *Contagious Feelings: Pauline Hanson and the Epidemiology of Affect*. Australian Humanities Review Retrieved on June 24, 2020 from http://australianhumanitiesreview.org/2001/12/01/contagious-feelings-pauline-hanson-and-the-epidemiology-of-affect/.

Godfrey, J. (1987). *A Philosophy of Human Hope*. Dordrecht, Boston and Lancaster: Martinus Nijhoff Publishers.

Goldstein, E. (2008). *Breaking down Barack Obama's Psychology of Hope and How It May Help You in Trying Times... A Blog About Mindfulness, Stress-Reduction, Psychotherapy and Mental Health*. Retrieved on April 6, 2020 from https://web.archive.org/web/20121110102512/http://www.mentalhelp.net/poc/view_doc.php?type=doc&id=28966&cn=110.

Good, M.-J. D., Good, B., Schaefer, C., & Lind, S. E. (1990). American Oncology and the Discourse on Hope. *Culture, Medicine and Psychiatry, 14*(1), 59–79.

Groopman, J. (2006). *The Anatomy of Hope: How People Prevail in the Face of Illness*. New York: Random House.

Güran-Aydin, P., & DeNora, T. (2016). Remembering Through Music: Turkish Diasporic Identities in Berlin. In A. L. Tota & T. Hagen (Eds.), *Routledge International Handbook of Memory Studies* (pp. 233–246). London: Routledge.

Hagen, T. (2019). *Living in the Merry Ghetto: The Music and Politics of the Czech Underground*. Oxford: Oxford University Press.

Hartley, N. (2009). *The Creative Arts in Palliative Care: The Art of Dying. Consent and Deceit in Pain Medicine*. The British Pain Society. Retrieved on April 22, 2020 from https://www.britishpainsociety.org/static/uploads/resources/files/2009_transcript__FINAL.pdf.

Hartley, N., & Ridley, A. (2016). Creativity, Discipline and the Arts at the End of Life: An interview with Nigel Hartley. Approaches: An Interdisciplinary [Special Issue]. *Journal of Music Therapy, 8*(1), 81–84. Retrieved on June 27, 2020 from http://approaches.gr/wp-content/uploads/2016/05/8-Approaches_812016_hartley-i20151129.pdf.

Hatfield, E., Carpenter, M., & Rapson, R. L. (2014). Emotional Contagion as a Precursor to Collective Emotions. In C. Von Scheve & M. Salmela (Eds.), *Collective Emotions: Perspectives from Psychology, Philosophy and Sociology*. Oxford: Oxford University Press.

Hauge, O. H. (2019). *Det er den draumen*. Oslo: Det Norske Samlaget.

Heidegger, M. (1962 [1927]). *Being and Time* (J. Macquarrie & E. Robinson, Trans.). New York: Harper & Row.

Hennion, A. (2007). These Things That Hold Us Together. *Cultural Sociology, 1*(1), 97–114.

Hennion, A., & Méadel, C. (1989). The Artisans of Desire: The Mediation of Advertising Between Product and Consumer. *Sociological Theory, 7*(2), 191–209.

Herwig, C., & Brune, A. (2019). *Hope in Their Hands: Refugee Children Share Their Keepsakes.* Unicef. Retrieved on March 24, 2020 from https://www.unicef.org/stories/hope-their-hands-refugee-children-share-their-keepsakes.

Hilbert, R. (1986). Anomie and the Moral Regulation of Reality: The Durkheimian Tradition on Modern Relief. *Sociological Theory, 4*(1), 1–19.

Hjørnevik, K., & Waage, L. (2018). The Prison as a Therapeutic Music Scene: Exploring Musical Identities in Music Therapy and Everyday Life in a Prison Setting. *Punishment and Society, 21*(4), 454–472.

Jedlowski, P. (2015). Memories of the Future. In A. L. Tota and T. Hagen (Eds.), *Routledge International Handbook of Memory Studies* (pp. 121–30). London: Routledge.

Jenkins, T. (2013). *Of Flying Saucers and Social Scientists: A Re-reading of When Prophesy Fails and of Cognitive Dissonance.* New York: Palgrave MacMillan.

Jewett, S. O. (1890). Miss Tempy's Watchers. In *Tales of New England.* Boston: Houghton, Mifflin and Co.

Joas, H. (2000). *The Genesis of Values.* Chicago: University of Chicago Press.

Jütten, T. (2019). Adorno on Hope. *Philosophy and Social Criticism, 45*(3), 284–306.

Keenan, B. (1993). *An Evil Cradling.* London: Vintage.

Keenan, B., & McCarthy, J. (2000). *Between Extremes: A Journey Beyond Imagination.* London: Black Swan.

King, M. L. Jr. (2005 [1960]) Creative Protest. *The Papers of Martin Luther King, Jr. Volume V: Threshold of a New Decade, January 1959-December 1960.* Berkeley, Los Angeles and London: University of California Press. Retrieved on 25 October, 2020 from https://kinginstitute.stanford.edu/king-papers/documents/creative-protest.

King, M. L. Jr. The Crisis in America's Cities. *The Atlantic.* Retrieved on July 11, 2020 from https://www.theatlantic.com/magazine/archive/2018/02/martin-luther-king-jr-the-crisis-in-americas-cities/552536/.

Kübler Ross, E. (2009 [1973]). *On Death and Dying.* London: Routledge.

Larkin, P. (1974). *High Windows.* London: Faber & Faber.

Lear, J. (2006). *Radical Hope: Ethics in the Face of Cultural Devastation.* Cambridge, MA: Harvard University Press.

Lehmann, D. (2016). Hope and Religion. In A. McKinnon & M. Trzebiatowska (Eds.), *Sociological Theory and the Question of Religion* (pp. 75–104). Taylor and Francis.

Lepore, J. (2020, June 15). The History of the Riot Report. *The New Yorker.* Retrieved on July 11, 2020 from https://www.newyorker.com/magazine/2020/06/22/the-history-of-the-riot-report.

Levitas, R. (2010 [1990]). *The Concept of Utopia.* Oxford: Peter Lang.

Lewis, G. (2017). "Let Your Secrets Sing Out": An Auto- Ethnographic Analysis on How Music Can Afford Recovery From Child Abuse. *Voices, 17*(2), n.p. Retrieved on March 21, 2020 from https://voices.no/index.php/voices/article/view/2346.

MacDonald, R., Burke, R. Birrell, R., DeNora, T., & Donohue, M. S. (Under Review). Our Virtual Tribe: Sustaining and Enhancing Community via Online Music Improvisation. *Frontiers in Psychology, 11,* 4076.

MacDonald, R., & Wilson, G. (2020). *The Art of Becoming: How Group Improvisation Works.* Oxford: Oxford University Press.

Mankowitz, Z. W. (2002). *Life Between Memory and Hope: The Survivors of the Holocaust in Occupied Germany.* Cambridge: Cambridge University Press.

McKesson, D. (2017). *On the Other Side of Freedom: The Case for Hope.* Penguin Books.

Merleau-Ponty, M. (2012). *Phenomenology of Perception.* London: Routledge.

Miller, D. (2010). *Stuff.* Cambridge: Polity.

Miyazaki, H., & Sweberg, R. (Eds.). (2016). *The Economy of Hope.* Philadelphia: University of Pennsylvania Press.

Mollison, J., & Gibson, M. (2015). See the Objects Refugees Carry on Their Journey to Europe. *Time Magazine.* Retrieved on March 24, 2020 from https://time.com/4062180/james-mollison-the-things-they-carried/.

Moreira, T., & Palladino, P. (2005). Between Truth and Hope: On Parkinson's Disease, Eurotransplantation and the Production of the 'Self'. *History of the Human Sciences, 18,* 55–82.

Morgan, M. (2016). The Responsibility for Social Hope. *Thesis Eleven, 136*(1), 107–123.

Mühlhoff, R. (2019). Affective Resonance. In J. Slaby & C. von Scheve (Eds.), *Affective Societies: Key Concepts* (pp. 189–199). London: Routledge.

Mukerji, C. (2009). *Impossible Engineering: Technology and Territoriality in the Canal du Midi.* Princeton: Princeton University Press.

Murad, N. (2019, July 31). My People Were Massacred Five Years Ago: The Genocide Continues. *Washington Post*.

Nietzsche, F. (1984). *Human, All Too Human*. London: Penguin Books.

Nilsen, A. (1999). Where Is the Future? Time and Space as Categories in Analyses of Young People's Images of the Future. *Innovation: The European Journal of Social Science Research, 12*(2) 175–194.

Novas, C. (2006). The Political Economy of Hope: Patients' Organizations, Science and Biovalue. *BioSocieties, 1*(3), 289–305.

Obama, B. (2004). *The Audacity of Hope: Thoughts on Reclaiming the American Dream*. New York: Crown.

Parker, I. (1997). *Psychoanalytic Culture*. London: Sage.

Pavlicevic, M. (2002). Dynamic Interplay in Clinical Improvisation. *Voices: A World Forum for Music Therapy, 2*(2).

Pavlicevic, M. (2010). Reflection: Let the Music Work: Optimal Moments of Collaborative Musicing. In B. Stige, G. Ansdell, C. Elefant, & M. Pavlicevic (Eds.), *Where Music Helps*. Farnham: Ashgate.

Pavlicevic, M., & Ansdell, G. (Eds.). (2004). *Community Music Therapy*. London: Jessica Kingsley Publishers.

Petersen, A. (2015). *Hope in Health: The Socio-Politics of Optimism*. Basingstoke: Palgrave Macmillan.

Petersen, A., & Wilkenson, I. (Eds.). (2014). The Sociology of Hope in Contexts of Health, Medicine and Healthcare [Special Issue]. *Health: An Interdisciplinary Journal for the Social Study of Health, Illness and Medicine, 19*(2), 113–118.

Polich, G., Iaccarino, M. A., Kaptchuk, T. J., Morales-Quezada, L., & Zafonte, R. (2018). Placebo Effects in Traumatic Brain Injury. *Journal of Neurotrauma, 1*, 35, 1205–1212. Retrieved on March 29, 2020 from https://www.ncbi.nlm.nih.gov/pubmed/29343158.

Prechtl, M. M. (1974). *Poster for G. Schirmer Music Company*. Retrieved on April 24, 2020 from https://www.lofty.com/products/vintage-1974-g-sch irmer-music-store-original-poster-featuring-beethoven-by-michael-prechtl-1-8xfhb.

Rasmussen, H. N., O'Byrne, K. K., Vandment, M., & Pl Cole, B. (2018). *Hope and Physical Health*. In M. W. Gallagher & S. J. Lopez (Eds.), *The Oxford Handbook of Hope* (p. 159). Oxford: Oxford University Press.

Reed, I. (2007). Why Salem Made Sense: Culture, Gender, and the Puritan Persecution of Witchcraft. *Cultural Sociology, 1*(2), 209–234.

Rolvsjord, R. (2005). Collaborations on Songwriting with Clients with Mental Health Problems. In F. Baker & T. Wigram (Eds.), *Songwriting: Methods,*

Techniques and Clinical Applications for Music Therapy Clinicians, Educators and Students (pp. 97–115). London: Jessica Kingsley.

Rolvsjord, T. (2016). *Resource-Oriented Music Therapy in Mental Health Care.* Gilsum, NH: Barcelona Publishers.

Rorty, R. (1999). *Philosophy and Social Hope.* London: Penguin Books.

Rose, N. (2007). *The Politics of Life Itself: Biomedicine, Power, and Subjectivity in the Twenty-First Century.* Princeton, NJ: Princeton University Press.

Rose, N., & Novas, C. (2005). Biological Citizenship. In A. Ong & S. Collier (Eds.), *Global Assemblages: Technology, Politics and Ethics as Anthropological Problems* (pp. 439–463). Malden, MA: Blackwell.

Ruud, E. (2002). Music as a Cultural Immunogen: Three Narratives on the Use of Music as a Technology of Health. In I. M. Hanken, S. G. Nielsen, & M. Nerland (Eds.), *Research in and for Higher Music Education: Festschrift for Harald Jørgensen* (pp. 109–120). Oslo: Norwegian Academy of Music.

Ruud, E. (2008). Music in Therapy: Increasing Possibilities for Action. *Music and Arts in Action, 1*(1), 46–60.

Ruud, E. (2010). *Music Therapy: A Perspective from the Humanities.* Gilsum, NH: Barcelona Publishers.

Ruud, E. (2020). *Toward a Sociology of Music Therapy: Musicking as a Cultural Immunogen.* Dallas, TX: Barcelona Publishers.

Sacks, O. (1991). *Awakenings.* London: Picador.

Schmid, W. (2017). Being Together—Exploring the Modulation of Affect in Improvisational Music Therapy with a Man in a Persistent Vegetative State—A Qualitative Single Case Study. *Health Psychology Report, 2*(5), 186–192. Retrieved on July 10, 2020 from https://www.termedia.pl/Being-together-Exploring-the-modulation-of-affect-in-improvisational-music-the rapy-with-a-man-in-a-persistent-vegetative-state-a-qualitative-single-case-stu dy,74,28789,1,1.html.

Scott, S. (2009). *Making Sense of Everyday Life.* Cambridge: Polity.

Sharp, G. (1973). *The Politics o Nonviolent Action.* Boston, MA: Porter Sargent Publishers.

Simons, D. J., & Chabris, C. (1999). Gorillas in Our Midst: Sustained Inattentional Blindness for Dynamic Events. *Perception, 28*(9), 1059–1074.

Skånland, M. S. (2011). Use of Mp3-players as Coping Resource. *Music and Arts in Action, 3*(2), 15–33.

Skånland, M. S., & Trondalen, G. (2014). Music and Grief: Norway After 22 July, 2011. *Voices: A World Forum for Music Therapy, 14*(2). Retrieved on April 16, 2020 from https://voices.no/index.php/voices/article/view/2230.

Slaby, J., & von Scheve C. (Eds.). (2019). *Affective Societies: Key Concepts.* London: Routledge.

Snyder, C. R. (1994). *The Psychology of Hope: You Can Get Here from There.* New York: The Free Press.

Snyder, C. R. (2002). Hope Theory: Rainbows in the Mind. *Psychological Inquiry, 13,* 249–275.

Snyder, C. R., Harris, C., Anderson, J. R., Holleran, S. A., Irving, L. M., Sigmon, S. T., et al. (1991). The Will and the Ways: Development and Validation of an Individual-Differences Measure of Hope. *Journal of Personality and Social Psychology, 60,* 570–585.

Snyder, C. R., Lopez, S. J., Shorey, H. S., Rand, K. L., & Feldman, D. B. (2003). Hope Theory, Measurements, and Applications to School Psychology. *School Psychology Quarterly, 18*(2), 122–139.

Snyder, C. R., Sympson, S. C., Ybasco, F. C., Borders, T. F., Babyak, M. A., & Higgins, R. L. (1996). Development and Validation of the State Hope Scale. *Journal of Personality and Social Psychology, 70,* 321–335.

Snyder, G., Rand, K. L., & Sigmon, D. R. (2018). Hope Theory: A Member of the Positive Psychology Family. In M. W. Gallagher & S. J. Lopez (Eds.), *The Oxford Handbook of Hope* (pp. 27–45). Oxford: Oxford University Press.

Solomon, G. F. (2002). The Development and History of Psychoneuroimmunology. In H. G. Koenig & H. J. Cohen (Eds.), *The Link Between Religion and Health: Psychoneuroimmunology and the Faith Factor* (pp. 31–42). Oxford, UK: Oxford University Press.

Stern, D. N. (2010). *Forms of Vitality: Exploring Dynamic Experience in Psychology and the Arts.* Oxford: Oxford University Press.

Stern, D. N. (2018 [1985]). *The Interpersonal World of the Infant.* London: Routledge.

Stige, B. (2002). *Culture-Centered Music Therapy.* Gilsum, NH: Barcelona Publishers.

Stige, B. (2004). Community Music Therapy: Culture, Care and Welfare. In M. Pavlicevic & G. Ansdell (Eds.), *Community Music Therapy* (pp. 91–113). London: Jessica Kingsley Publishers.

Stige, B. (2015). The Practice Turn in Music Therapy Theory. *Music Therapy Perspectives, 33*(1), 3–11.

Swidler, A. (2001). What Anchors Cultural Practices? In T. Schatzki, K. K. Cetina, & E. von Savigny (Eds.), *The Practice Turn in Social Theory* (pp. 74–92). London: Routledge.

Taylor, R. (2018). Relationship, Not Intervention: A Palliative Physician's Perspective. In A. Goodhead & N. Hartley (Eds.), *Spirituality in Hospice Care: How Staff and Volunteers Can Support the Dying and Their Famiies* (pp. 57–83). London: Jessica Kingsley Publications.

Terkel, S. (2003). *Hope Dies Last: Keeping the Faith in Difficult Times.* New York: The New Press.

Terpe, S. (2014). Negative Hopes: Social Dynamics of Isolating and Passive Forms of Hope. *Sociological Research Online.* Retrieved on March 25, 2020 from https://journals.sagepub.com/doi/full/10.5153/sro.3799?casa_token= ppAC6_V2nkAAAAA%3AIlDeGczr7_6ciZfSMkxpdPU1agACHQHf0L XN62fHgkO1UH0riejmkix_K6RajJfjd2XryyxUVyE.

Thompson, E. (2017). *Waking, Dreaming, Being: Self and Consciousness.* New York: Colombia University Press.

Tota, A. L. (2001). Homeless Memories: How Societies Forget Their Past. *Studies in Communication Sciences, 1,* 193–214.

Tota, A. L. (2004). Ethnographying Public Memory: The Commemorative Genre for the Victims of Terrorism in Italy. *Qualitative Research, 4*(2), 131–159.

Tota, A. L. (2005). Counter Memories of Terrorism: The Public Inscription of a Traumatic Past. In M. Jacobs & N. Hanrahan (Eds.), *The Blackwell Companion to the Sociology of Culture* (pp. 272–285). Oxford: Blackwells.

Tota, A. L. (2016). Dancing the Present: Body Memory and Quantum Field Theory. In A. L. Tota & T. Hagen (Eds.), *Routledge International Handbook of Memory Studies* (pp. 458–472). London: Routledge.

Trondalen, G. (2016). *Relational Music Therapy: An Intersubjective Perspective.* Dallas, TX: Barcelona Publishers.

Twiddy, I. (2015). *Cancer Poetry.* Basingstoke: Palgrave Macmillan.

von Goethe, J. W. (2010 [1792]). Experiment as a Mediator of Subject and Object. *In Context #24* (Fall), 19–23.

Vygotsky, L. S. (1978). Mind in Society: The Development of Higher Psychological Processes. In M. Cole, V. John-Steiner, S. Scribner, & E. Souberman (Eds.), Cambridge, MA: Harvard University Press.

Vygotsky, L. (2004). Imagination and Creativity in Childhood. *Journal of Russian and East European Psychology, 42*(1), 7–97.

Waite, T. (1993). *Taken on Trust.* London: Hodder and Stoughton.

Warhurst, C., van den Broek, D., Hall, R., & Nickson, D. (2012). Great Expectations: Gender, Looks and Lookism at Work. *International Journal of Work, Organisation, and Emotion, 5*(1), 72–90.

Wartolowska, K., Judge, A., Hopewell, S., Collins, G. S., Dean, B. J., Rombach, I., et al. (2014). Use of Placebo Controls in the Evaluation of Surgery: Systematic Review. *British Medical Journal, 348*.https://doi.org/10.1136/bmj.g3253.

Weber, M. (2011). *The Protestant Ethic and the Spirit of Capitalism*. Oxford: Oxford University Press.

White, J. W. (2017). *Midnight in American: Darkness, Sleep and Dreaming During the Civil War*. Chapell Hill: University of North Carolina Press.

Winther-Lindqvist, D. A. (2017). Hope as Fantasy: An Existential Phenomenology of Hoping in Light of Parental Illness. In B. Wagoner, I. Bresco de Luna, & S. Awad (Eds.), *The Psychology of Imagination: History, Theory and New Research Horizons*. Charlotte, NC: Information Age Publishing Inc.

Witkin, R. W. (1974). *The Intelligence of Feeling*. Portsmouth, NH: Heinemann Educational Publishers.

Witkin, R. W. (1995). *Art and Social Structure*. Cambridge: Polity Press.

Yolen, J. (2003). The Radiation Sonnets: For My Love, in Sickness and in Health. *Family & Community Health, 29*(1), 68.

Younge, G. (2013). *The Speech: The Story Behind Martin Luther King's Dream*. Chicago: Haymarket Books.

Name Index

Subject Index

© The Editor(s) (if applicable) and The Author(s), under exclusive
license to Springer Nature Switzerland AG 2021
T. DeNora, *Hope*,
https://doi.org/10.1007/978-3-030-69870-6

Printed in the United States
by Baker & Taylor Publisher Services